M000078071

LOST
CIVILIZATIONS

pil

Publications International, Ltd.

Images from Shutterstock.com and Wikimedia Commons

Contributing writer: Lisa Brooks

ISBN: 978-1-63938-306-1

Manufactured in China.

8 7 6 5 4 3 2 1

Let's get social!

 @Publications_International

 @PublicationsInternational

www.pilbooks.com

TABLE OF CONTENTS

TABLE OF CONTENTS

AFRICA

THE PYRAMIDS: WHY AND HOW?

The Egyptian pyramids may be some of the most recognizable—and the most magnificent—manmade structures in the world. In fact, the largest of the structures, the Great Pyramid of Giza, is the only one of the original Seven Wonders of the World still standing, despite it also being the oldest of the wonders. Originally encased in limestone, the Great Pyramid stood 481 feet tall when it was completed, and even after vandalism and erosion reduced it to its present height of 454 feet, it held the title of tallest manmade structure in the world for more than 3,000 years.

For much of those millennia, humans not only marveled at the mammoth stone structures, but they also wondered why and how they were created. Without machines or technology of any kind, the ancient Egyptians somehow managed to create amazingly distinctive buildings that became a symbol of the country and have more than stood the test of time.

FIT FOR A GOD

Pyramids in Egypt were built from the beginning of the Old Kingdom until the fourth century A.D., but the peak of their construction was in the Fourth Dynasty, with construction significantly slowing by the Sixth Dynasty. At the dawn of the Old Kingdom, kings held a revered place in Egyptian society.

They were believed to be divinely appointed by the gods themselves, and even thought to have godlike qualities. A king was seen as the representation of Horus, the god who serves as protector of the god Ra. But when that king died, he was said to become the god of the dead, Osiris.

This association between the gods and the kings of Egypt dictated how the kings were treated after death. Since kings were akin to gods, it was in everyone's best interest to treat them accordingly. Simply burying a deceased king in the ground would not do. And since the Egyptians believed that part of the king's spirit, known as the "ka," remained with his body, he needed to be buried with gold, food, and even furniture for the afterlife.

So, the Egyptians came up with the perfect tribute for their godlike kings—structures so majestic and lofty that they would serve as reminders of the kings' glory for millennia to come: pyramids. The unique shape of these monolithic mausoleums was not by accident. Their smooth, angled sides symbolized the rays of the sun, and helped the deceased's spirit ascend upward to the gods. Inside, the mummified king would be placed in a chamber with everything he might need for the afterlife, and nearby, smaller pyramids and tombs were reserved for relatives, wives, or officials of the king.

A MONUMENTAL UNDERTAKING

But the question of "why" the pyramids were built may not have piqued as much curiosity amongst archeologists, historians, and even amateur Egyptologists as "how" they were built.

The Great Pyramid alone contains some 2.3 million blocks of stone, each weighing approximately 2.5 tons, that needed to be cut from quarries and transported to the building site. Even by modern standards, the assembly of such a structure would be challenging. So how did the ancient Egyptians accomplish such a task?

Just as with any huge undertaking, it took practice, patience, and a multitude of people working together for a common goal. The first pyramids weren't the nearly perfect triangles we see today at Giza; rather, they were built by adding on to simple, rectangular tombs called *mastabas*. The first rudimentary pyramids had a regular rectangular mastaba base, with "steps" of ascending layers to the top. These soon gave way to the smooth-sided structures we're familiar with today.

Papyrus texts have been discovered which detail the planning that went into the construction projects, which required more than just precise architecture. First, plenty of people were needed to carry out the construction. While many used to believe that slaves were used to build the pyramids, recent evidence seems to suggest that most workers were local farmers who were unable to grow anything during the Nile flooding season. At least 10,000 men were required to build the pyramids at Giza, and records show that enough cattle, sheep, and goats were kept nearby to provide the workers with 4,000 pounds of meat every day. Far from being slaves, the pyramid builders were probably more well-fed than anyone else in the region!

STONES, SLEDS, AND THE SUN

Assembling the workers to build the pyramids must have been the easiest part of the project. The hard part was actually constructing the colossal structures. Most of the stones used for the pyramids came from local quarries. While no one is certain how each stone was cut so precisely, theories suggest that workers used copper chisels and saws, along with tools like wooden levels or string, to cut the blocks.

Once a block was ready, moving it even a few feet would've taken some tremendous effort. The Egyptians probably used large sleds to transport the rocks, dragging them over sand that had been dampened with water. The water would reduce the friction of the sand, making it easier for fewer people to drag the sled across the desert. Once at the pyramid site, it is likely that the workers pulled the stones up a series of ramps, and perhaps used levers to make the process easier. Using these techniques, it took somewhere between 20 and 30 years to complete the pyramids at Giza.

One of the most interesting, and still mysterious, facts about the Great Pyramid is that it was very precisely aligned along the cardinal points—north, south, east, and west—to within one tenth of a degree. Even today, researchers aren't sure how the ancient Egyptians were able to achieve such accuracy. Some believe they may have used the stars for guidance, while others think the sun may have helped, especially if the pyramid builders tracked the sun during the fall or spring equinox.

Of course, one of the most outlandish, but often cited, theories concerning the construction of the pyramids is the notion that they may have extraterrestrial origins. With their mammoth size, precision construction, and seemingly endless ability to withstand the ravages of time, perhaps it's not hard to understand why this idea has taken hold of imaginations. But it also diminishes the amazing accomplishments of a group of innovative, intelligent, and hard-working human beings who constructed some of the most impressive monuments in history. Aliens may play a role in the movies, but the earthly human truth of the pyramids is much more extraordinary.

THE LOST CITY OF THINIS

Thousands of years ago, ancient Egypt was divided into two regions: Upper Egypt and Lower Egypt. Named for their locations in relation to the south-to-north flow of the Nile River, Upper Egypt (which was upriver) was the southern portion of the land, whereas Lower Egypt (downriver) was the northern portion. Perhaps even the ancient Egyptians found this up-and-down geography a bit confusing, because by 3100 B.C., the two regions had unified, ushering in the Archaic or Early Dynastic Era of Egypt.

This era was also known as the Thinite Period, named after the first capital city of the newly unified Egypt, Thinis. According to Manetho, an Egyptian priest who authored a chronology of the kings of ancient Egypt, the pharaoh who united the two regions was a member of a tribal group based in Thinis called the Thinite Confederacy. This pharaoh, named in various sources as either Menes or Narmer, declared the city to be the capital of the newly created Egypt, and it remained the capital into the First or Second Dynasty of Egypt.

A RELIGIOUS CENTER

It may be assumed that archeologists have uncovered a plethora of artifacts from this important city, but the truth is just the opposite: the city of Thinis has never been found. Along with the writings of Manetho, Thinis was mentioned in many ancient manuscripts, including the religious text *The Book of Going Forth by Day*, often known by its more common name, *The Egyptian Book of the Dead*. Through the recordings of ancient peoples, we can be certain that Thinis existed; but its location remains a mystery to this day.

While its location may be unknown, most scholars believe it was probably situated close to Abydos, one of the oldest cities in Egypt. Records show that the city possessed great wealth, and provided food, weapons, and troops to the pharaoh's army. Thinis was also a religiously significant city, containing a temple to the god of war, Anhur. Anhur's consort, the goddess Mehit, was also worshipped in the city. But gods and goddesses were not the only recipients of the Egyptians' reverence. According to the Book of the Dead, Thinis itself was associated with the afterlife, existing as a celestial city in the heavenly realm.

FARMERS AND TAXES

The great wealth enjoyed by the city of Thinis continued even after the city of Memphis became the capital. This was recorded in tax documents of the era, which showed that Thinis was taxed gold, silver, cattle, and honey on an annual basis. The city was also required to pay 65 sacks of grain yearly, compared to the three sacks that were paid by nearby Abydos. This suggests that farming and agriculture were hugely important to Thinis, and probably made up the majority of its industry.

Could this large focus on agriculture explain why Thinis has never been found? Some archeologists believe so. Farmers often lived in structures made of easily perishable materials like wood and mud, whereas stronger materials like stone were reserved for temples and tombs. If Thinis, as the first city in the first era of a unified Egypt, was lacking many stone structures, it's possible that it simply disappeared under the sands of the desert. But its religious significance can't be forgotten, either; certainly the city had a stone temple or two, even if most of its residents were simple farmers. Either way, Thinis grew less and less vital as the eras of Egypt moved on, and by the Roman Period in 30 B.C., it was all but forgotten. With all of the written evidence we have, one thing is certain: The city of Thinis existed, somewhere. Perhaps one day someone will stumble upon its sand-shrouded remains in the Egyptian desert. But in the meantime, we can only guess where its location may be, and ponder how this modest farming city sparked the beginnings of the great kingdom of Ancient Egypt.

ABYDOS: CITY OF THE DEAD

In 2021, archeologists made an unusual discovery in the Egyptian city of Abydos, which lies about 280 miles south of Cairo. The researchers uncovered a 5,000-year-old brewery, believed to have been capable of making more than 5,900 gallons of beer at a time. This immense brewery, possibly the oldest ever discovered in the world, provided a steady stream of beer to the kings of Abydos and was used for many sacrificial rites and rituals.

The rites and rituals in the ancient city were especially important to the people of Abydos, who established the city around 3100 B.C. as a necropolis for the earliest royalty of the first and second dynasties of Egypt. This "city of the dead" counted the jackal-headed god, Khenti-Amentiu, as its protector. But by the fifth dynasty, beginning around 2465 B.C., reverence for Khenti-Amentiu gradually transformed into a worship of Osiris, the god of life, death, and the afterlife.

CULT OF OSIRIS

Abydos became a destination for pilgrims in the cult of Osiris, who believed that the god himself was buried within the city. Pious Egyptians would travel to the city, desiring to one day be buried as close to the tomb of Osiris as possible. Records of journeys to Abydos undertaken by wealthy families are found all throughout Egypt. But even those who could not afford the travel or the cost of burial in the city found a way to leave a piece of themselves in Abydos: archeologists have found thousands of *stelae*, or stone slabs, engraved with the names and titles of Egyptians who could not make a final trip to the city. The stelae were also engraved with prayers to Osiris, an effort to make sure the deceased person would be close to the god in the afterlife.

Over the centuries, pharaohs built and expanded a temple to Osiris in the city, eventually calling it the Great Temple of Osiris. It was here that Egyptians would gather to worship Osiris and his counterpart, Isis. Every year, pilgrims would gather for a celebration of their god, carrying a likeness of Osiris from the temple to where his tomb was believed to be, in a great, elaborate procession. The jubilant participants would then carry the likeness back to the temple, passing many private and royal chapels that were located along the processional route.

SETI I AND THE MOTHER OF POTS

The Great Temple of Osiris was important to the people of Abydos, but it was not the only temple they built in the city. One of the best known, and surviving, temples is the Temple of Seti I, also known as the Great Temple of Abydos. Built by the pharaoh Seti I around 1300 B.C., the temple was built to not only memorialize Seti himself, but to honor the pharaohs of previous dynasties. This was accomplished with a long gallery featuring a relief of Seti and his son, Ramesses, making offerings to the cartouches of 76 of their predecessors. Known as the Abydos King List, the gallery is especially valued by modern researchers because it is the only known record of many of the kings of the seventh and eighth dynasties of Egypt.

Abydos is also known for *Umm el Qa'ab*, the royal cemetery where the kings of the first and second dynasties were buried. Umm el Qa'ab means "Mother of Pots," and it was so named because the site is littered with pottery shards and other items that were left by religious pilgrims. Archeological excavations that began in the 1970s discovered inscriptions on many of the objects that suggested Egyptian writing had become more advanced much earlier than originally assumed.

The temples and city of Abydos continued to be expanded, revamped, and used until the thirtieth dynasty of Egypt, which lasted until 343 B.C. Today, while the Great Temple of Osiris has been reduced to ruins, many of the ancient structures from this civilization still stand, giving researchers a valuable look into the lives of ancient Egyptians. It is no wonder that Abydos is considered one of the most important archeological sites in the world.

AKHENATEN: THE CITY OF LIGHT

In 1912, a German archeological team discovered a 19-inch-tall, 44-pound, limestone and stucco bust in what had once been the workshop of a 14th-century B.C. sculptor named Thutmose. The bust became one of the most recognizable pieces of ancient art in the world, depicting one of the most famous women of the ancient world: Nefertiti. The piece was found in the deserted city of Akhenaten, also known as Amarna, which had been founded around 1346 B.C. by Nefertiti's husband, Pharaoh Akhenaten.

The pharaoh—who, before the fifth year of his reign, was known as Amenhotep IV—had some unusual ideas that were previously unheard of in ancient Egypt. As king, he was entrusted with preserving *ma'at*, or harmony and balance, in Egypt. Traditionally, an important part of ma'at was maintaining the rites and rituals that served to honor the gods and goddesses. At first, the pharaoh continued these practices; but in the fifth year of his reign, he abolished the polytheistic ancient Egyptian religion and created his own monotheistic religion based on the sole worship of Aten, a minor deity who personified the light of the sun. The pharaoh's new name, Akhenaten, meaning "the horizon of the Aten," or "effective for the Aten," reflected his new devotion to the deity.

Aten represented the life-giving light of the sun, possessing no weaknesses or harmful traits. By merely existing, Aten caused all things to exist. The god may have been a "minor" deity in his polytheistic past, but to Akhenaten, Aten was supremely powerful on his own. The pharaoh didn't believe that such a god should be worshiped in temples that were created for other gods; so, he decided to build a city devoted to his new monotheism.

A NEW CAPITAL

The city, Akhenaten, was situated along six miles of the east bank of the Nile River, between the cities of Memphis and Thebes. Completed around 1341 B.C., the city immediately became the capital of the eighteenth dynasty of Egypt. Akhenaten was laid out in four distinct areas, which today are known as the north city, central city, southern suburbs, and outskirts.

The north city was the location of the Northern Palace, where guests were received and the royal family resided. The palace was constructed without a roof, a common feature of the buildings in the city, which was seen as a gesture of welcome for Aten. The central city was the location of administration buildings and two important temples to Aten, the Great Temple and the Small Temple. Wealthy residents lived in large estates in the southern suburbs, whereas peasants and farmers occupied the outskirts of the city.

A SINGULAR PROBLEM

While the city of Akhenaten flourished under the pharaoh's rule, the same cannot be said for the rest of Egypt. Akhenaten's singular focus on the worship of Aten distracted him from many affairs of state, and as his reign progressed, he seemed to care less and less for his kingly duties. And while he may have meant well by creating his monotheistic religion, Egypt's economy suffered greatly because of it. Temples were key sources of economic activity, employing thousands of people and engaging in local trades and industry. When the pharaoh imposed worship of only Aten, many temples were forced to close, while others lost much of their support. Even Egypt's military lost clout during Akhenaten's reign, and the country lost its good standing with lands at its borders.

When Akhenaten died after 17 years of rule, his son, the famous Tutankhamun, reestablished polytheism in Egypt, reopened the temples that had been closed, and moved the capital to Thebes, the city of his birth. The city of Akhenaten struggled to survive for at least a decade but was eventually abandoned. Perhaps the empty city could have one day found life again, had it not been for one of Tutankhamun's successors, Horemheb.

DOWNFALL AND DISCOVERY

Horemheb had been a military general under Akhenaten, and while he served the king well, he greatly disagreed with his monotheistic religious policies. When Horemheb became pharaoh, he wanted no record of Akhenaten's kingdom. He ordered the city razed, and used the bricks and stones leftover for his own projects.

It is no wonder that the ruins of Akhenaten sat undiscovered for thousands of years. It was not until the 18th century that archeologists began excavating the ancient capital, uncovering foundations of temples, monuments, and a collection of 300 cuneiform tablets known as the Amarna Letters. These letters include official documents from Akhenaten's reign as well as correspondence with foreign nations. Archeologists also discovered the king's tomb, although Akhenaten himself was nowhere to be found, possibly a victim of grave robbers.

The famous bust of Nefertiti, which happily survived Horemheb's destruction of the city, is now known worldwide as a symbol of feminine beauty. Ironically, very little is definitively known about Akhenaten's royal wife, yet she has become one of the most instantly recognizable faces of the ancient world. Hopefully, the city in which she once lived will continue to reveal secrets of its complicated and controversial past.

THE OLD KINGDOM: THE AGE OF THE PYRAMIDS

Without a doubt, one of the first things that comes to mind when we hear the word "Egypt" is pyramids. Although ancient pyramids have been found in many parts of the world, including China, Mexico, India, and Greece, the Great Pyramid at Giza is perhaps the most famous example of this type of architecture. For more than 3,000 years, this pyramid held the record for the tallest manmade structure in the world, rising 481 feet over the dusty Egyptian desert.

So it's no wonder that the Old Kingdom of Egypt, a period spanning from approximately 2700 B.C. to 2200 B.C., and encompassing the Fourth Dynasty during which the pyramids were built, is also commonly known as the Age of the Pyramids or the Age of the Pyramid Builders. It was during this time that pharaoh Sneferu devised innovative ways to construct the monolithic structures, helping to perfect the art and science of pyramid-building.

Along with the Fourth Dynasty, the Old Kingdom includes the Third, Fifth, and Sixth dynasties, as well. Historical records of this period are scarce; however, scholars have been able to piece together a history of the time period thanks to architectural monuments, like the pyramids, and the many inscriptions left behind by their builders. Because of this, historians like to say that the history of the Old Kingdom is literally "written in stone."

IMHOTEP'S ARCHITECTURE

The Old Kingdom traditionally begins with the Third Dynasty of Egypt, a period of growth and change for the civilization. It was during this time that the once independent states of Egypt came to be ruled under a centralized government located in the capital of Memphis. The Third Dynasty also saw changes in architecture, politics, and religion, which would all serve to transition Egypt into the height of the Old Kingdom.

The Third Dynasty is also when King Djoser, who reigned for more than 20 years, began many building projects in the village of Saqqara, including the first pyramid ever constructed in Egypt. The pyramid was designed by Djoser's architect, Imhotep, who built the stepped pyramid to be used as a tomb for the king. Imhotep is often credited with being the first builder in Egypt to construct tombs out of stone. Prior to his designs, the structures were often created using mud bricks; but Imhotep was determined to create a lasting tribute to his king, building a stone pyramid and surrounding temples, and creating a model that would be followed by many dynasties after.

SNEFERU AND THE THREE PYRAMIDS

This era of change led to the Fourth Dynasty of Egypt, largely regarded as the most prosperous period during the Old Kingdom. The first king of the Fourth Dynasty, Sneferu, followed Imhotep's footsteps and commissioned several pyramids, but his structures relied on a bit of trial and error. Sneferu changed some of Imhotep's designs on his first try, aiming to construct a true pyramid and not a "stepped" pyramid, but ultimately these changes resulted in a *collapsed* pyramid. Today, what remains of this structure, which is located in Meidum and is known as the "false pyramid," looks more like a tower sitting atop a pile of gravel.

Sneferu's next pyramid, now known as the Bent Pyramid, also hit a bit of a snag. As workers were assembling the structure, they realized that the angle of the walls was too steep. So halfway through the project, the angle of the walls was changed from 55 degrees to 43 degrees. This gave the pyramid its distinctive "bent" appearance. Undeterred, Sneferu started on his last pyramid, now called the Red Pyramid due to the reddish limestone which was used for its construction. After so many false starts, the Red Pyramid, built on a solid base with walls rising at a 43-degree angle, finally became the first true pyramid in Egypt.

KHUFU: HATED OR LOVED?

Sneferu was a well-liked and much respected king, who established a stable, strong government and was careful with his use of resources. According to inscriptions found on ancient stone tablets, the king was even prone to calling his subjects "brother," and was generous and compassionate, even to prisoners. His rule was the beginning of a golden age in the Old Kingdom, which continued once his son, Khufu, began to reign.

In contrast to his father, Khufu was described as a "tyrant" by the ancient Greeks, who claimed that the king oppressed and enslaved the people. However, Egyptian texts, such as the

Westcar Papyrus, a document discovered in 1824 by a British traveler named Henry Westcar, seem to refute this claim, praising Khufu and his treatment of his subjects. The Greek impression of Khufu as an oppressive tyrant seems to stem from a specific highlight of the king's reign: the construction of the Great Pyramid.

According to the ancient Greek writer Herodotus (who is sometimes called "The Father of History" but is also known for exaggerating his stories), Khufu forced hundreds of thousands of men to work on his pyramid for months at a time, with no rest. This story gave the ancient Greeks, and even some modern historians, the idea that slaves were used to build the Great Pyramid. But Egyptian texts and physical evidence uncovered over hundreds of years of excavation tell a different story. Today, most scholars agree that Khufu was not only an admired ruler, but that the people who built his pyramid were treated well. More than likely, they were either paid for their labor or volunteered as a community service. Some people also helped with the construction during the Nile's annual flood, when their usual farming work was impossible.

A COLOSSAL MONUMENT AND A SMALL PYRAMID

Khufu's sons Djedefre and Khafre were the next kings to rule during the Fourth Dynasty of the Old Kingdom, with Djedefre making an important pronouncement about Egyptian royalty. Djedefre, who ruled between 2566 and 2558 B.C., was the first king of Egypt to associate the kingship with the sun god Ra, adding "Son of Ra" to the royal title. His brother Khafre took over in 2558 B.C., and is often credited with the construction of the Great Sphinx of Giza. The largest monolithic statue in the world, the Sphinx depicts the face and head of a king, with the body of a reclining lion. Because the statue is aligned perfectly with Khafre's pyramid complex, most scholars agree that his is the face depicted by the Sphinx. But some believe the statue may have been commissioned by Djedefre in honor of his father, and the face is that of Khufu. Either way, the Sphinx is rivaled only by the Great Pyramid when considering symbols of the Old Kingdom.

After a brief reign by Baka, son of Djedefre, Khafre's son, Menkaure, became king in 2532 B.C., after his father's death. During his reign, Menkaure began building his own pyramid and temple complex, just as his father and grandfather had done, but the resources necessary for a project as colossal as the Great Pyramid had dwindled by this time. Foreshadowing the Old Kingdom's eventual decline, Menkaure's pyramid was much less grand than previous structures. Even with its smaller size, the pyramid was unfinished by the time of Menkaure's death, even after 30 years of reigning as king. His successor, Shepseskaf, completed the project; but, as there were not enough resources left to create another grand pyramid, after his death Shepsekaf himself was interred in a modest burial chamber.

THE SONS OF RA

The death of Shepsekaf signaled the end of the Fourth Dynasty and ushered in the Fifth. The Fifth Dynasty saw a slight shift in the power dynamic between Egyptian citizens and kings, who, prior to the Old Kingdom, were believed to be human manifestations of gods. But Djedefre's declaration that the king was a "son of Ra," effectively reduced the power of the king from that of a god to that of a son of a god. Priests began to wield more influence, and the Egyptian people worshiped the god Ra directly, instead of venerating the king as a representative of their god.

So much significance was given to the god Ra during the Fifth Dynasty that it is often called the "Dynasty of the Sun Kings." No longer was the focus on the creation of grand pyramids; rather, temples were constructed not for the worship of royalty, but for citizens to worship the sun god. The first king of this time period, Userkaf, is best known for overseeing the construction of the Temple of the Sun at Abusir, the first tangible sign that the influence of the Egyptian kings was waning.

Userkaf's son, Sahure, ruled after his father, and counted the first Egyptian expedition to the land of Punt as one of his greatest achievements. Although Egypt's subsequent trade with Punt would be greatly important, Sahure made a much less significant contribution—by way of Egyptian architecture—that would later become one of the country's characteristic symbols. It was Sahure who first made use of "palmiform" columns in his Temple to the Sun. This well-known architectural style, which features a column topped with the shape of a palm frond, is instantly recognizable as distinctly Egyptian.

The worship of Ra and diminishing power of the king continued throughout the Fifth Dynasty, until 2414 B.C., when Djedkare Isesi took the throne. For the first time during the dynasty, a king decided not to honor the sun god with a temple. Djedkare Isesi reduced the number of priests in his kingdom and strengthened

Egypt by renewing ties with Punt and revitalizing the economy. Some scholars believe that the king's decision to depart from worship of the sun god was because he was an early follower of the cult of Osiris, which would eventually replace the cult of Ra as the most popular deity worship in Egypt.

THE COLLAPSE OF THE KINGDOM

Whatever the reason, this departure from previous traditions served to reduce the king's influence even further. By the time the Sixth Dynasty began with the reign of Teti in 2345 B.C., the idea that only kings should build elaborate monuments and tombs was falling by the wayside. Now, local government officials and administrators constructed their own tombs and temples, bringing an end to hundreds of years of royal customs. Teti was the first king to be assassinated, possibly by his successor, Userkare, in a plot that would have been shockingly unthinkable in previous dynasties.

The assassination of Teti was a portent of the collapse of the Old Kingdom. Instead of a king with huge influence over the entire country, local administrators, called *nomarchs*, wielded most of the power. Instead of kingly, royal dynasties, local dynasties of nomarchs were created, as local officials passed their titles on to their descendants. Struggles within the country, and even civil wars, sporadically broke out, but the end of the Old Kingdom was signaled by a drought in the 22nd century B.C. Without a strong ruler to lead the people of Egypt through the hardship, the country was beset with famine. The nomarchs could only attempt to help their own communities, as they lacked the resources to do more.

As the once grand Old Kingdom came to an end, Egypt descended into a period of political struggle, disorganization, and conflict. But while the Age of the Pyramid Builders was over, the impressive monuments, art, inscriptions, and temples they left behind have assured that the Old Kingdom of Egypt will never be forgotten.

THE GREAT SPHINX

In ancient mythology, a sphinx was a creature with the head of a human and the body of a lion. To the Greeks, the sphinx had the face of a woman and eagle's wings on its lion-body, and was most notably depicted in the myth of Oedipus. Cunning and ruthless, she required anyone who wished to pass by safely to answer a riddle or face death. To the Egyptians, the sphinx was usually shown as having the face of a man, and was seen as less merciless and more benevolent. But the two mythologies shared the idea of the sphinx as a guardian, and the creature was often featured at the entrance to tombs or temples.

The most well-known version of a sphinx is the Great Sphinx of Giza, built around 2500 B.C., which sits within the famous complex of pyramids on the Giza Plateau. Standing approximately 66 feet tall and spanning a length of 244 feet from its lion paws to tail, the Sphinx is one of the largest and oldest monolithic statues in the world. The original name of the statue is unknown, and scholars are not even certain that the ancient Egyptians considered it a sphinx. But most agree that the monument is an homage to a pharaoh, and a representation of the divine.

THE FACE OF A KING

While the face of the statue has succumbed to weathering and vandalism—the nose was deliberately broken off sometime between the third and tenth centuries A.D.—most archeologists agree that the statue was built to represent the king Khafre. Khafre's father, Khufu, built the Great Pyramid, the largest pyramid in Egypt. Khafre's pyramid was ten feet shorter than his father's, but, not to be outdone, he also added a much more elaborate surrounding complex, which included the Great Sphinx.

Workers created the monolith by carving out the bedrock of the plateau. This actually served a twofold purpose, as the stone from the area was used to construct the pyramids and other structures in the area. Some researchers believe that the head of the Sphinx was carved first, out of a naturally occurring feature called a "yardang." This is when the combination of wind, dust, and sand carve a protuberance of rock, which can sometimes resemble a person, animal, or building. It's possible that this large natural rock formation already resembled a human head; the imaginations of the rock carvers took over from there. Archeologists estimate that it took 100 people about three years to carve out the bedrock and create the statue.

NEGLECT AND RESTORATION

After the collapse of the Old Kingdom, the Great Sphinx was ignored and forgotten for hundreds of years. It enjoyed a short period of restoration in 1400 B.C., when Thutmose, the son of the pharaoh Amenhotep II, claimed to have a dream in which the Sphinx called to him and asked him to restore it. If he did so, the dream Sphinx said, Thutmose would become pharaoh. Thutmose obeyed the dream, and not only became pharaoh, but also introduced a sphinx-worshipping cult to Egypt.

But soon after, the Sphinx was once again disregarded, left to sit alone in the desert. Eventually, it was buried in sand up to its shoulders. It wasn't until 1930 that Egyptian archeologist Selim Hassan was able to dig away thousands of years of neglect and finally free the Sphinx to display its grand monolithic stature again. Restoration and preservation has been ongoing since, with archeologists determined to maintain the impressive structure and protect this piece of history.

There are many unanswered questions about the Sphinx, including whether the face is that of Khafre or someone else, and what significance the statue had to its builders. No one even knows who broke off the nose of the statue. Perhaps it is fitting that there is so much we don't know about the Sphinx, since riddles feature so prominently in the origin of the creature. The monument may have left us with many riddles, but generations to come will continue to ponder them. Meanwhile, the Great Sphinx will sit, silently and majestically, on the desert plateau, holding on to its secrets.

THE LOST KINGDOM OF BENIN

The 2018 film *Black Panther* enthralled audiences with its
depiction of the fictional African kingdom of "Wakanda."
The fantastical country contained such stunning wealth and
technology that its leaders hid its location from the rest of the
world, lest their riches be stolen or misused. Depicted as a
kingdom ahead of its time, a place like Wakanda could only be
found in the imaginations of filmmakers, right?

Perhaps not. While Wakanda itself was entirely a place of fiction, the African continent did once contain a kingdom that was
so far ahead of its time that it became the envy of the European
world. Known as the Kingdom of Benin, or the Edo Kingdom,
evidence of its founding by the Edo people of southern Nigeria
dates back to the 11th century. The city was established within
dense rainforest, providing its inhabitants with animals for food,
plants for medicines, and wood for construction. And construct
they did: over the next several hundred years, Benin expanded
to encompass around 500 separate villages.

WALLED IN

More impressive than the expansion of the city, however, were
the walls that surrounded it. According to archeologists, the
main city of Benin and its outlying villages were surrounded by nearly 10,000 miles of earthwork banks and ditches,
which would've taken the people of Benin a total of about
150 million hours of digging to complete. The walls and city
itself may also have been planned and laid out according to
fractal geometric design. Fractals are continuous patterns that

demonstrate self-similarities across different sizes and scales. Examples in nature would include snowflakes, ferns, or sea-shells, which exhibit obvious repeating patterns, on small or large scales. In Benin, some researchers believe fractal designs were planned out in the walls, the villages, and even each individual house in the city, giving the entire kingdom a sense of mathematical symmetry.

The city contained some notable features that were, at the time, unheard of in many other parts of the world, including a sewer system beneath the streets that carried storm water away, wells for each house that provided fresh water, and "streetlights" fueled by palm oil that helped travelers find their way through the area at night. Benin became a hub of creativity and culture, with artists working in bronze, iron, and ivory to create wall plaques, carvings, and sculptures, including life-sized bronze heads of their *Obas*, or kings.

EUROPEAN FRIENDS AND FOES

In 1485, the first Europeans stumbled upon the kingdom of Benin when Portuguese explorers led by João Afonso de Aveiro found the city, sprawling and thriving, nestled in the rainforest. Soon, Benin was no longer an isolated city hidden by vegetation; it became a hugely popular destination for European traders, who raved about the city back home, noting its wealth, beautiful art, friendly citizens, and sophisticated government. In fact, it was said that Benin was so clean, prosperous, and well-managed, that crime was non-existent, and people lived in houses with no doors.

For several centuries, Benin and European traders enjoyed a civil and pleasant relationship, with the kingdom offering palm oil, ivory, and pepper in exchange for the guns brought from Europe. But by the late 1800s, British colonial influence began to crowd its way into Benin. While the people of the kingdom were always happy to trade with the Europeans, it soon became clear that British traders to the city were intent upon colonization. The Oba would not hear of it, and in 1896 he cut off trade with the British empire. When a British-led expedition, intent on reestablishing contact, tried to enter the city in January of 1897, they were ambushed and attacked, with only two British men managing to escape.

LOST TO THE JUNGLE

Sadly, this was the beginning of the end for the kingdom of Benin. The British soon sent a "punitive expedition" of 1,200 men to the city, and over the course of nine days, Benin was sacked, looted, and burned. The Oba was captured and exiled. Many of the looted artifacts wound up in museums and universities, but recently there has been an effort to begin returning the items to Nigeria.

Today, a new Benin City stands where the ancient kingdom once thrived, but none of the old city's distinctive features remain. The fractal houses, the expansive walls, the clever streetlights—all have been lost to time and the surrounding jungle. Perhaps one day some enterprising explorer will discover a bit of earthen ditch or excavate the foundation of an unusual ancient house, and the world will be reminded of the remarkable lost city that was ahead of its time.

D'MT AND KESKESE: ANCIENT AND ENIGMATIC

In 2003, archeologists in Eritrea made an astounding discovery when they unearthed the skeleton of a young woman, which was dated to be more than a million years old. The remains were believed to show a link between early hominids and modern humans, giving scientists a small glimpse into our ancient history.

The discovery also served as a reminder that Eritrea and its surrounding areas are no strangers to antiquity. Much of the region's history has been well documented and studied, but there are still unknowns to explore, such as the mysterious kingdom of D'mt and its ritual site of Keskese.

CITIES OF MYSTERY

Once located in what is now Eritrea and northern Ethiopia, little is known about the city of D'mt—sometimes known as Damot—but historians believe it existed between the 10th and 5th centuries B.C. The ancient civilization may have called the city of Yeha, in northern Ethiopia, its capital. A temple to the moon god Almaqah still stands in Yeha, alluding to the formation of the city at a time before Islam or Christianity had made its way to the region. D'mt was an agricultural society, and the people constructed plows and developed irrigation systems to grow their crops, and also fashioned tools and weapons out of iron.

D'mt was believed to have been influenced by its South Arabian neighbors, including the area of present-day Yemen. Evidence of this fact is found in the nearby archeological site of Keskese, once the seat of ritual practices in D'mt. Stone inscriptions featuring the name of a South Arabian king have been discovered at the site, but the city is mostly known for its "stelae," a collection of stone pillars and obelisks which range in length from about 22 feet to almost 30 feet. Remains of walls and terraces have also been found, as well as remnants of tools and pottery.

Thanks to these bits of historic evidence, we can assume the people of D'mt spent their days tending to their millet fields, focusing on metalwork, or constructing the obelisks that marked their ritual site. But we may never know why, in the 5th century B.C., D'mt and Keskese simply disappeared. Their abrupt ending made way for the Kingdom of Aksum, which arose to great power in the early 1st century. But historians still have much to learn about these two enigmatic cities, which left behind precious few clues to tell us about their once thriving societies.

SONGHAI: MIGHTY AFRICAN EMPIRE

What began as a small kingdom founded in the 9th century by fishermen along a bend of the Niger River eventually became the most important region in West Africa. This was the Songhai Empire, also called the Songhay, which dominated the western half of the African continent in the 15th and 16th centuries.

But before the Songhai Empire could rise to ultimate power, it had to overtake the prevailing Mali Empire, a kingdom that had been prospering since the 13th century. The Mali Empire controlled both local and international trade in gold and spices, but the Songhai controlled the transport of goods along the river, making them troublesome neighbors for Mali. When civil wars in the mid-1400s began to weaken Mali's influence, the rulers of Songhai saw an opportunity to expand their territory.

MERCILESS EXPANSION

In 1468, King Sunni Ali of Songhai ordered a military campaign of territorial expansion, making use of Songhai's river-borne naval fleet—the only naval fleet in North Africa. Sunni Ali conquered the Mali Empire, cementing Songhai's path to power in the region. The king gained a reputation for ruthlessly striking down his enemies, earning the nickname "Sunni the Merciless," and quickly expanded Songhai into many provinces that were each overseen by governors he appointed. By 1473, the Songhai Empire controlled most of the centers of trade in the area, keeping a tight rein on the caravans of salt, cloth, horses, ivory, and spices that traversed the Sahara.

Sunni Ali was succeeded by his son, Sunni Baru, who, in turn, was overthrown by Mohammad I. Mohammad I, who was the first in the region to popularize the use of the title *Askia*, meaning "ruler," oversaw what would be the largest expansion of the Songhai Empire. By the early 1500s, the capital city of Gao was home to 100,000 people, and Songhai's territory spanned from the Senegal River in the west, to central Mali in the east, to the salt mines of Taghaza in the north.

A GRAIN OF SALT

In the late 1500s, the sultan of Morocco, Ahmad al-Mansur, took notice of Songhai's impressive salt mines, which were a vital part of the trade routes they controlled. The sultan demanded that Askia Daoud, the ruler of Songhai at that time, pay tax revenues for the salt mines. Askia Daoud attempted to satisfy al-Mansur's demands by offering large quantities of gold, but the sultan wasn't appeased. In late 1590, al-Mansur sent 4,000 men to attack Songhai. In what became known as the Battle of Tondibi, al-Mansur's forces clashed with 40,000 men of the Songhai army. While there is no doubt that al-Mansur's men were greatly outnumbered, the Moroccans had a huge advantage: gunpowder. The Songhai Empire may have been expansive, but they had only spears and arrows for defense.

The Moroccans quickly won the battle, and the once formidable Songhai Empire was gradually absorbed and vanquished by the Moroccans. Its downfall was astonishingly fast and sadly absolute: within two years, Songhai, the largest, most powerful kingdom in West Africa for more than 125 years, simply crumbled and vanished, demonstrating that the mighty can, most certainly, fall.

THE TREASURES OF TIMBUKTU

It is quite common in our modern age to equate "Timbuktu"—today a city in the West African country of Mali—with a
far-off location or a long trip. Throwing out an exasperated, "I
had to drive from here to Timbuktu!" tells a listener just how
long and arduous a journey was, even if only in the mind of
the speaker. The fact that we still, in the 21st century, equate
Timbuktu with faraway lands speaks to the enigmatic history
of this city, and of our ongoing curiosity of ancient cultures.

Timbuktu has long been considered a mysterious place. In fact,
a 2006 U.K. survey found that a third of young Britons wrong-
ly believed the city to be fiction. It's hard to blame anyone for
this misunderstanding, as stories of Timbuktu have often been
awash in fantastical anecdotes that spark imaginations.

Of course, the truth of Timbuktu is not nearly as opulent as
the rumors; but that doesn't mean that the city's history is any
less impressive. Archeologists have found evidence of human
occupation of the region around Timbuktu that dates back to
the Iron Age, but the city was not formally established until
medieval times. At first, the location was used as a seasonal
camp by salt traders; but by the early 12th century, the area
became a permanent hub for caravan trade of all kinds. Many
of these traders decided to put down roots in the area, and
soon, Timbuktu was a thriving and prosperous city, where
travelers from the west brought gold to exchange for salt from
the east.

THE MIDAS TOUCH

According to many scholars, an event in the early 1300s first ignited the swirling rumors of Timbuktu's wealth and helped to spread its fame far and wide. By this time of the century, the Mali Empire was the most powerful kingdom in West Africa. Mali was already well known for the wealth of its ruler, Mansa Musa, who is still often called one of the wealthiest people in history. A devout Muslim, Musa decided to undertake a pilgrimage to Mecca, or *hajj*, in 1324, a journey of 2,700 miles. Musa wasn't alone, however: his entourage comprised an astounding 60,000 men. This included 12,000 slaves who carried four pounds of gold each, plus 80 camels carrying bags of gold dust. The entire procession was outfitted in Persian silks, and heralds carried gold staffs.

This display of wealth was obvious enough, but Musa didn't simply show off—he also shared what he had. All along the journey, Musa made stops to share his gold with other pilgrims and those in need, and was said to have financed the building of mosques in many cities along the way. Some accounts say that Musa handed out so much gold on his pilgrimage that by the time he reached Cairo, the price of the metal had dropped greatly.

Musa's pilgrimage to Mecca became fodder for myth and legend, spawning a persistent rumor that his nearly endless supply of gold came from the city of Timbuktu. In reality, the gold had come from mines west of the city, but that didn't stop the story of the gold-laden kingdom of Timbuktu from taking on a life of its own. Like the mythical El Dorado of South America,

Timbuktu was thought of as a hidden, mysterious city, a place that explorers and adventure-seekers might stumble upon in the middle of the desert. Soon, people in other parts of the world were dreaming of a secret paradise brimming with gold in the far-off, exotic land. These rumors of opulent palaces and gold-lined streets reached the ears of Europeans in the 1300s, as the bubonic plague began to ravage the continent. Imagining a warm, desert paradise full of treasure surely would have been a preferable distraction to the realities of disease, and may explain why the stories of Timbuktu at the time were so fanciful and flamboyant.

AFRICANUS IN AFRICA

Gold or no gold, Musa annexed the city of Timbuktu when he returned from his pilgrimage, making it part of the prosperous Mali Empire. But Musa wasn't the only character who helped place Timbuktu on the world stage. Another was Leo Africanus, a diplomat and author best known for his book *Description of Africa*. Africanus was born al-Hasan ibn Muhammad al-Wazzan in Andalusia, Spain, in 1485. The area was under Muslim rule until the reconquest of Spain by King Ferdinand and Queen Isabella in 1492, when the rulers exiled all Muslims in the country, including Africanus's family, who moved to Fes, Morocco.

Africanus was an intelligent man who not only traveled throughout North Africa extensively, but also spoke Latin and Italian, in addition to his native Arabic. After impressing Pope Leo X with his knowledge and intellect, Africanus converted to Christianity and took the Latin name Johannes Leo de Medicis, or, in Italian, Giovanni Leone. The pope commissioned him to write a book about the continent of Africa, which was published in Italian in 1550. *Description of Africa* went on to become hugely popular and was eventually translated into French, Latin, and English.

Africanus's book, which was one of the only resources available to Europeans wishing to learn about Africa, included several descriptions of Timbuktu. The author described the "rich king" of the city, detailing his many gold objects, "some whereof weigh 1300 pounds." Africanus also described the prosperous resources the city possessed, including food, livestock, and an abundance of "learned men." Europeans were once again fascinated and intrigued by this city which had already captured their imaginations centuries earlier. But this time, they had a first-hand account from someone who had visited the city in person, instead of simply rumors and gossip.

WEALTH OF INFORMATION

While Africanus did write of the gold and prosperity within Timbuktu, he highlighted another aspect of the city that gave it what many scholars consider its true source of wealth: its love of books. In fact, the 15th and 16th centuries are considered Timbuktu's "Golden Age," but not because of literal gold; rather, these centuries were marked by a rise in education, literacy, and a trade in books that gave Timbuktu a reputation in the Islamic world as a center of learning and culture.

During this time, Timbuktu was home to around 200 *maktabs*, or Quranic schools, which attracted students from all over the region. Some historians estimate that at the height of its Golden Age, Timbuktu was crowded with 25,000 scholars. Many of them were also scribes, creating manuscripts of religious, philosophical, historical, and scientific works. Thousands of texts were written, and hundreds of thousands were gathered through a bustling book trade. Manuscripts ranged from those written by local astronomers, mathematicians, religious scholars, and other experts, to texts translated from famous historical figures like Plato and Hippocrates.

In addition to the maktabs, Timbuktu created *madrasahs*, which were informal but religious institutions modeled after European medieval universities, where scholars gave lectures on their subjects of expertise. The city so prized learning and knowledge that even visitors passing through were seen as possible sources of new information. Guests were warmly welcomed and treated like royalty, in the hopes that they could share new wisdom with the citizens of Timbuktu. Even more than gold, Timbuktu considered literacy and books to be symbols of its power and wealth.

END OF THE GOLDEN AGE

Unfortunately, this power and wealth was not long-lived. In 1591, Morocco invaded Timbuktu in order to make it the new capital of its empire. The scholars of Timbuktu were disbanded and scattered: some were imprisoned or even executed for disloyalty to the new rulers, while others were exiled or escaped to nearby countries. The Golden Age of Timbuktu came to an abrupt end.

The city's once lively book trade was over, but those who remained in Timbuktu during Moroccan rule understood the importance of the variety of manuscripts the city had collected over the years. In an effort to preserve this knowledge and keep it safe from those who might attempt to destroy it, families began hiding copies of everything they could get their hands on. Texts were hidden in cellars, buried underground, lowered into wells, and concealed behind walls, where they were kept safe like precious treasure, sometimes for centuries.

It was the 1800s by the time the first Europeans finally braved exploration of the Sahara—enduring malaria, hunger, and other dangers—to reach the long-imagined city of Timbuktu. By then, the city's Golden Age was long past. When stories of the realities of the legendary city reached Europe, they were much less impressive than what the centuries of rumors had led some to believe. No streets of gold, no opulent palaces, no silk-adorned kings. French explorer René Caillié, the first European to journey to and from Timbuktu, described it as desolate and quiet, a city which "exuded the greatest sadness." In modern times, the city has struggled with droughts, increasing desertification, and an influx of terrorists and extremists, which has often led governments to discourage travel to the region.

Despite its modern-day struggles, the Western world often still thinks of Timbuktu as a mysterious, hidden city of gold. But as the city itself once understood, its true sources of wealth were the books, education, and knowledge it possessed. Today, historians are searching for the real hidden treasure of Timbuktu and working to restore its greatest legacy: its collection of nearly 700,000 manuscripts. Three of the city's original madrasahs—Djinguereber, Sidi Yahya, and Sankore—are still standing today and are collectively known as the University of Timbuktu. These structures, and the manuscripts they contain, are reminders of this once-wealthy kingdom, and the knowledge that it yearned to gather and share with the world.

TIMGAD: LOST AND FOUND

The ancient city of Pompeii is famous not only for its destruction after the eruption of the volcano Mount Vesuvius, but also for its remarkably well-preserved state. Modern day visitors can wander the same streets Pompeii residents once walked, and see a glimpse of the past frozen in time. This famous city is visited by millions of people a year; but few have heard of another well-preserved ancient kingdom that many liken to Pompeii: the city of Timgad.

Timgad was founded by the Roman Emperor Trajan around the year 100, in what is now northern Algeria. The emperor gave the city the rather unwieldy name *Colonia Marciana Ulpia Traiana Thamugadi*, in honor of his family—his mother, Marcia; sister, Ulpia Marciana; and father, Marcus Ulpius Traianus. The last part of the name, *Thamugadi*, was a word used by the indigenous Berber tribes in the area, and is believed to mean "peak" or "summit." This reflects the city's location in the Aurès Mountains of Algeria, at just over 3,000 feet above sea level.

GRIDLOCK

Timgad was originally created to house Roman military veterans, and to act as a show of strength against the local Berbers. Since it was founded on an unsettled area of land, the Romans were able to construct the city however they wanted. This resulted in an impressive feat of ancient urban planning, with streets laid out in a grid system around two main thoroughfares: the decumanus maximus, which ran from east to west, and the *cardo*, which ran north to south. A stately sandstone gate known as the Arch of Trajan was constructed at the west end of the *decumanus maximus*, featuring an 11-foot-wide central arch. The city also included a library, a basilica, several bathhouses, an amphitheater, and a temple dedicated to the god Jupiter which rivals the size of the Pantheon in Rome.

For several hundred years, Timgad's residents enjoyed peace and prosperity. The city became a center for commerce and trade, and expanded from its original small population of Roman military veterans to more than 15,000 citizens from across the Roman Empire. The city grew so much that it could no longer be contained within the orderly grid of its original design, causing it to spill out into a much more haphazard pattern.

LOST TO THE DESERT

But the peace didn't last long: in the 5th century, Germanic Vandals sacked the city, looking to expand their own influence in North Africa. Weakened, Timgad was then nearly destroyed by Berbers from the surrounding mountains. Although it was repopulated for a short time, the city was completely abandoned by the 8th century, left to the whims of the winds and sands of the desert. Timgad was slowly buried underneath more than three feet of dry ground, and forgotten for a thousand years.

It wasn't until 1765 that a British explorer named James Bruce reached the neglected city and described it in a book about his North African travels. Still, it took more than a hundred years for others to take note of the once-remarkable city, and in 1881, French archeologists began excavating Timgad. They discovered that the dry air and sand of the desert had perfectly preserved much of the city, giving them the rare chance to study an ancient civilization. By the 1960s, most of Timgad had been uncovered, revealing what was once a vibrant city. Nearly every building in the area is still clearly outlined by the remains of walls and foundations. The precisely laid out streets are paved with large limestone slabs, some of which clearly display worn chariot tracks. Private houses and villas are adorned with intricate mosaics, hinting at the wealth of the city's residents. A visit to the upper seats of the amphitheater provides a view of the entire city, including the public forum, bathhouses, and the imposing Arch of Trajan.

WHAT'S OLD IS NEW

One thing that surprises archeologists about this ancient city is how familiar it feels in our modern age. Researchers were clearly able to see how the growing population of Timgad had caused it to branch out into nearby locations, with newer buildings constructed on the outskirts of the city in a less ordered fashion than the central area. This is not unlike most cities found in the world today: a downtown area contains the highest concentration of businesses and people, whereas growth leads to less-organized suburban areas. Timgad may have been the first city to feature "suburban sprawl."

Today, Timgad is a UNESCO World Heritage Site, where visitors can explore a bit of ancient history. Although Timgad's citizens are long-gone, they left behind some advice in the form of a Latin motto engraved on the steps to the large basilica:

Venare, lavari, ludere, ridere, occ est vivere. "Hunt, bathe, play, laugh, that is life." It would seem that during its glory days, Timgad provided comfort, prosperity, and contentment to its lucky inhabitants. While Pompeii may have had a more dramatic ending, Timgad deserves some attention for being one of the best-preserved ancient cities in the world.

ALEXANDRIA'S FABLED LIBRARY

By far the most famous library in history, the Library of Alexandria held an untold number of ancient works. Its fiery destruction meant the irrecoverable loss of a substantial part of the world's intellectual history.

The cities of ancient Mesopotamia (e.g., Uruk, Nineveh, Babylon) and Egypt (e.g., Thebes, Memphis) had cultivated archives and libraries since the Bronze Age, but the idea for a library as grand as Alexandria did not occur in Greek culture until the Hellenistic Age, when Alexander the Great's conquests brought both Greece and these former civilizations under Macedonian rule. Previous Greek libraries were owned by individuals; the largest belonged to Aristotle (384–322 B.C.), whose work and school (the Lyceum) in Athens were supported by Alexander.

When Alexander died suddenly in 323 B.C., his generals carved his empire into regional dynasties. The Hellenistic dynasties competed with each other for three centuries (until each was in turn conquered by either Rome or Parthia). Each dynasty desired cultural dominance, so they invited famous artists, authors, and intellectuals to live and work in their capital cities. Alexander's general Ptolemy, who controlled Egypt, decided to develop a collection of the world's learning, along with a research center, the *Mouseion* (the Museum, or "Temple of the Muses"), where scholars on subsidy could study and add their research to the collection. This idea may well have come from Demetrius of Phaleron (350–280 B.C.), Ptolemy's advisor and the former governor of Athens, who had been a pupil at the Lyceum, but the grand project became one of the hallmarks of the Ptolemaic dynasty. Under the first three Ptolemies, the Museum, a royal library, and a smaller "daughter" library at the Temple of Serapis (the Serapeum) were built and grew as Alexandria became the intellectual, as well as commercial, capital of the Hellenistic world.

Egypt and Alexandria offered the Ptolemies distinct advantages for accomplishing their goals. Egypt was not only immensely rich, which gave it the wealth to purchase materials and to bring scholars to Alexandria, but it was the major producer of papyrus, a marsh reed that was beaten into a flat surface and made into scrolls for writing and copying. Alexandria was also the commercial hub of the Mediterranean, and goods and information from all over the world passed through its port.

SO MANY SCROLLS, SO LITTLE TIME

Acquiring materials for the libraries and Museum became somewhat of an obsession for the Ptolemies. Although primarily focused on Greek and Egyptian works, their interests included translating other works and traditions into Greek. Among the most important of these efforts was the production of the Septuagint, a Greek version of the Jewish scriptures. Besides employing agents to scour major book markets and to search out copies of works not yet in the library, boats coming into Alexandria were required to declare any scrolls on board. If they were of interest, the scrolls were confiscated and copied, and the owners were given the copies and some compensation.

Ptolemy III (285–222 B.C.) may have acquired Athens' official state collection of the plays of Aeschylus, Sophocles, and

Euripides in a similar way—putting up 15 talents of silver as a guarantee while he had the plays copied, then foregoing the treasure in favor of keeping the originals. Whether or not this is true, it speaks to the value he placed on getting important works and the resources he had at his disposal to do so.

Alexandria's efforts were fueled by a fierce competition with the Hellenistic kingdom of Pergamum (modern Bergamo, Turkey), which created its own library. Each library sought to claim new finds and to produce new editions, leading at times to the acquisition of forgeries and occasional embarrassment. Alexandria finally tried to undercut its rival by cutting off papyrus exports, but Pergamum perfected a method for making writing material out of animal skins (now called "parchment" from the Latin *pergamina*) and continued to build its holdings. Eventually, however, Alexandria got the upper hand when the Roman general Marcus Antonius (Mark Antony) conquered Pergamum and made a present of its library to his lover, the Ptolemaic Queen Cleopatra.

Estimates as to the number of volumes in the Alexandrian library ranged wildly even in antiquity, generally between 200,000 and 700,000. Estimates are complicated by the fact that it isn't clear whether the numbers originate from works or scrolls: Some scrolls contained one work, some multiple works, and long works like the *Iliad* took multiple scrolls. Over time, a complex cataloguing system evolved, which culminated in a bibliographic survey of the library's holdings called the *Pinakes*. The survey was put together by the great Hellenistic scholar and poet Callimachus of Cyrene (305–240 B.C.). Unfortunately, this important work only exists in fragments today.

BURNING DOWN THE HOUSE

The Royal Library and its holdings were accidentally set aflame in 48 B.C. when Caesar (who had taken Cleopatra's side in her claim to the throne against her brother) tried to burn his way out of being trapped in the port by opposing forces. Further losses probably occurred in A.D. 271 when Emperor Aurelian destroyed part of the Museum while recapturing Alexandria from Queen Zenobia's forces. The "daughter" library of the Serapeum was finally destroyed by Christians under Emperor Theodosius near the end of the 4th century. But by then, much of the contents (like the contents of other great civic libraries of antiquity) had decayed or found their way into other hands, leaving the classical heritage scattered and fragmented for centuries. Much later, Christians dramatically blamed the burning of the library holdings on Muslim conquerors. Although this made for a good story, the legendary contents of the library were already long gone.

THE BADARIAN PEOPLE

Up until about 12,000 years ago, all the humans on earth relied on hunting and gathering for food and shelter. This way
of life required people to live as nomads, roaming to different
locations in search of animals and plants for sustenance.
While these early peoples harnessed the use of fire, created
tools, learned to preserve their food, and had a wealth of
knowledge about plant life, they were never able to settle in
a single location, as they were always forced to travel to their
sources of food.

But then, in a drastic change of lifestyle that archeologists now
dub the "Neolithic Revolution," humans developed agriculture. With the advent of farming, humans were able to settle
in permanent locations for the first time in their history. Now
that crops could be constantly cultivated and livestock continually raised, there was no reason to wander. Civilizations were
founded, villages and cities were established, and the world's
population increased.

DISCOVERY ALONG THE NILE

In Upper Egypt, the Badarian culture is the earliest example of an agricultural civilization in the region. Named for
its discovery in El Badari, a town which is approximately
120 miles northwest of modern Luxor, the Badarian culture arose around 5000 B.C. and was at its pinnacle from
4400 to 4000 B.C. It was discovered in 1922 by English
archeologists Guy Brunton, who would go on to become
the assistant director of the Egyptian Museum in Cairo,

and Gertrude Caton-Thompson, one of the first women to significantly contribute to the field of archeology. Brunton and Caton-Thompson uncovered around forty settlements, located in a 19-mile stretch along the eastern bank of the Nile River. Their excavation gave researchers insight into an ancient culture that flourished during the Predynastic Era of Egypt.

Although none of the Badarian structures remain, archeologists were able to uncover storage pits and holes for posts, some of which still had the remains of wooden stumps. The storage pits are believed to have been used to store the wheat, barley, lentils, and flax that the Badarian people cultivated. Pottery, carved figurines, arrowheads, and jewelry were also found in the area. Along with agriculture, the Badarian people practiced fishing and also raised domesticated animals like sheep, goats, and cattle. The animals were an important part of the Badarian culture, and were often laid to rest in ceremonial burial sites.

At least 600 human burial sites were also found during the excavation, with bodies usually interred facing west. The Badarian people buried their dead wrapped in reed mats or animal hides, and placed items in the graves including ceramics, jewelry, fine cloth, amulets, or even cosmetic palettes. Some people were also buried with figurines of female mortuary figures or fertility idols.

PARTICULAR POTTERY

Many of the tools used by the Badarian people were quite simple, but Brunton and Caton-Thompson were impressed and surprised by the quality and uniqueness of the culture's pottery. In fact, it is the pottery that sets the Badarian culture apart from other cultures of the time. The pottery was fashioned with red Nile clay, and often featured a black interior and rim. But the most distinctive detail was an unusual, spiraled rippling effect which covered either the entire surface of a piece, or part of it.

Archeologists are still unsure of what sort of tool was used to create the decorative ripples, but the majority of the pottery found in the area displays the unique texture. Badarian pottery is also notable for its thin, sometimes almost sharp, edges, which were found nowhere else during the Predynastic Era.

Other items found in the region, such as turquoise, shells, and basalt vases, indicate that the Badarian people traveled to and traded with other cultures in the area. But for the most part, the Badarian people were settled and content to be at home in their civilization along the Nile. Thanks to their embrace of agriculture—and as the first people in Upper Egypt to do so—the Badarian culture was able to leave behind a wealth of information about their ancient lifestyle and practices.

THE MERCHANTS OF NORTH AFRICA

History enthusiasts may recall the story of the military general Hannibal, who famously led his army and herd of North African war elephants through Spain and across the Alps into Italy. Although a risky and costly strategy, it was also a great surprise to his enemies, who probably never expected an army, and certainly not elephants, to make such a journey through the mountains. Hannibal's well-planned battles led him to many victories in Italy, and he controlled much of the southern half of the country for many years. But this was not the end of the wars that plagued the region, and eventually, Hannibal was forced to return to the city of his birth: Carthage.

Hundreds of years before Hannibal's famous trek through the mountains, Carthage was a small Phoenician settlement located on what is now the Tunisian coast. Founded around 814 B.C., the site was chosen by the Phoenicians due to its access to the Mediterranean Sea and proximity to trade routes.

While the Phoenicians had many settlements in the region, the vast majority of them were small, with populations rarely topping out over 1,000 people. Carthage, however, became the exception. The location of the settlement, with its ideal climate, arable land, and accessibility to the sea and trade routes, made it immensely popular. Within a century of the first settlers arriving, Carthage had grown to a population of 30,000.

THE CRÈME DE LA CRÈME

The founders of the city had chosen its location wisely. Carthage became an important center for trade between Africa and the rest of the ancient world. It was known for its luxurious goods, including jewelry, carved ivory, food, wine, spices, and rare purple dye extracted from the shells of marine snails. Beds, cushions, textiles, and mattresses produced in Carthage were considered premium indulgences, and those who were unable to afford them attempted to copy the furniture and linens that they so coveted. Carthage also controlled much of the tin and silver that was mined in North Africa and southern Spain. Tin was an essential component in the creation of bronze, making it an especially lucrative metal and providing the settlement with further revenue.

The prosperous city was surrounded by walls that were said to be 32 feet thick and more than 40 feet high in some areas. These walls, which ran for 21 miles around the city, enclosed four separate residential areas as well as marketplaces, theaters, artisan workshops, religious districts, towers, and a necropolis. Outside the walls were the agricultural lands, where, according to the writings of a Carthaginian named Mago, landowners grew olive, pomegranate, almond, fig, and date palm trees; raised cattle, sheep, and poultry; kept bees and bottled honey; and engaged in winemaking.

INDEPENDENCE AND EXPANSION

For a time, the people of Carthage remained loyal to their Phoenician background and customs, and the city sent annual tributes to Tyre, which had been the powerful main city of the Phoenician civilization when Carthage was founded. But Tyre's strength and influence started to wane just as Carthage grew in wealth and power, and the settlement began wishing for independence. Sometime around 650 B.C., Carthage gained its independence and set its sights on expanding its new empire. Perhaps emboldened by their growing prosperity, the Carthaginians sought out new sources to supplement their trade network and strengthen their economy.

Carthage set itself apart from other Phoenician settlements, not only by its success and population, but also its desire for military conquest. Unlike other Phoenician city-states, which rarely engaged in conflicts over territory, Carthage became a strong military power in the western Mediterranean. The docile Phoenician colonies, including Hadrumetum, Utica, and Kerkouane, were quickly absorbed into the Carthaginian empire. Carthage then gained control of coastal Africa, from Morocco to Libya, and the islands of Sardinia, Malta, Mallorca, Ibiza, and the western half of Sicily. The Iberian Peninsula was the next to bow under their control, with some of the largest and most important Carthaginian settlements established there.

A GROWING THREAT

But Carthage was not the only "superpower" emerging in the Mediterranean during this time. Rome, founded in 753 B.C., had also begun as a small settlement like Carthage, but was growing in influence on the Italian peninsula to the north. In 509 B.C., the two civilizations signed the first of several peace treaties in an attempt to lay out boundaries and protect interests. The two empires differed in their strategies for territorial expansion, with Carthage focusing on the sea and controlling trade routes, and Rome concentrating on acquiring more of mainland Italy.

Carthage soon controlled much more territory than Rome, and established a powerful navy to protect itself from the pirates and rivals who wished to get their hands on Carthaginian wealth. Mercenaries from Celtic tribes and African allies soon joined forces with Carthage, who began to see a threat from the Greeks. The Greeks had begun to establish their own Mediterranean trade routes, vying for dominance over the Carthaginians, especially on the island of Sicily. War soon broke out between the two groups, who were each expert in the art of maritime navigation, well familiar with the waters of the Mediterranean, and determined to gain control of Sicily. Eight wars, known as the Sicilian Wars, were fought over the span of more than 200 years.

THE PYRRHIC WAR

The last of the Sicilian Wars is known as the Pyrrhic War, named so after Pyrrhus of Epirus, a Greek king who fought both the Romans and the Carthaginians. In 278 B.C., Pyrrhus was asked by several Greek cities in Sicily to come to the island and drive out the Carthaginians. The king obliged, and for a time, it seemed he would be victorious. He captured many of the strongest Carthaginian cities in Sicily, and was even planning to name his son heir to the Sicilian kingdom. But the king did not anticipate how stubbornly the Carthaginians would hold on to their last major Sicilian city, Lilybaeum. Carthage offered Pyrrhus money and ships if he would sign a peace treaty, but the king would only agree if Carthage turned over control of the island. Carthage refused, and the siege of the well-fortified and well-armed Lilybaeum continued. Try as he might, Pyrrhus could not wear down the Carthaginians, and he began to suffer heavy losses.

The king then made the mistake of forcing the Greeks, who had asked him to come to the island, to pay for his rein-forcements and repairs. When they resisted, he treated them ruthlessly, even executing two Greek rulers on false charges of treason. The Greeks lost their faith in Pyrrhus, and after three years in Sicily, the king gave up and led his navy away to mainland Italy. According to some accounts, as he was leav-ing the island, he proclaimed prophetically, "What a wrestling ground we are leaving, my friends, for the Carthaginians and the Romans."

THE FIRST AND SECOND PUNIC WARS

Around 275 B.C., the Romans became the protectors and leaders of all of Italy. This, of course, included the island of Sicily, which the Carthaginians preferred to control due to its ideal location within their trade routes. Tensions between the two civilizations began to rise, and Carthage placed its navy in the Strait of Messina, the narrow channel of water that sepa-rates the eastern tip of Sicily from mainland Italy. Eventually, the animosity between the enemies rose, and war broke out in 264 B.C. Known as the First Punic War, this conflict lasted 23 years and resulted in Rome gaining control of Sicily—the first administrative territory outside of mainland Italy that would become a part of the Roman Empire.

But the conflicts between Carthage and Rome were far from over. In 219 B.C., a Carthaginian army led by Hannibal captured the pro-Roman city of Saguntum in the Iberian Peninsula. This led to a declaration of war by the Romans, kicking off the Second Punic War. Hannibal took his large army, along with 37 war elephants, from the Iberian coast in the west to the Rhone River in the east, reaching the foot of the Alps in the autumn of 218 B.C. Fighting frigid, snowy weather, difficult terrain, and hostile native tribes, the army crossed the mountains. After losing many men, and most of the elephants, to hunger, exhaustion, and falls from the slippery mountain heights, the army finally reached Italy.

Although Hannibal had early successes and even controlled parts of Italy for a time, Roman forces eventually found victory in 203 B.C., and Hannibal sailed back to Carthage. Rome also gained control of Iberia, delivering a blow to the Carthaginians' main source of manpower for their armies. Finally, Rome took the fight directly to the heart of Carthage, attacking settlements in Tunisia. The Romans agreed to a peace treaty in 201 B.C., but Carthage had lost everything it had worked so hard to acquire, save its North African city.

FINAL WAR AND DESTRUCTION

But soon, even the city of Carthage would be a thing of the past. In 149 B.C. the Third Punic War, and the last, was fought, after Roman senator Cato the Elder expressed the opinion that Carthage should be "destroyed." Despite the fact that the Carthaginians had been stripped of most of their resources and wealth, the city put up a fierce fight when the Romans invaded. Amazingly, they held off the Romans for three years, although they no doubt realized it was a lost cause. In 146 B.C., Roman general Scipio Aemilianus ruthlessly defeated the city of Carthage, ordering it to be burned, razed to the ground, and plowed over. He killed or enslaved 50,000 Carthaginians.

Julius Caesar eventually rebuilt the city as a Roman seaport, and over the centuries, Carthage saw many different occupying forces, including the Vandals, Byzantines, Muslims, and Crusaders. But perhaps the empire is best known for the exploits of its military leader, Hannibal. Interestingly, Hannibal's surname, Barca, was derived from the Punic word *barqa*, meaning "lightning." A fitting name for a Carthaginian general who staged one of the most risky and surprising military campaigns in history, on behalf of an empire that once shone brilliantly and brightly.

HERACLEION: LOST TO THE SEA

The famous "lost city of Atlantis" was a fictional island first mentioned in the works of Plato. The philosopher wrote about the island in 360 B.C. in his works *Timaeus* and *Critias*, where he used the imaginary civilization to represent an arrogant naval power that attacks Athens, Plato's idea of a "perfect society." Athens is able to fight off the attack, and Atlantis, which loses favor with the gods, is submerged into the sea. It was a minor tale in Plato's vast collection of works, but it immediately took hold of the imaginations of those who read it.

In fact, not everyone who read about Atlantis was convinced that it was imaginary. Since Plato's first mention of the island more than two thousand years ago, scholars have scoured the planet, hoping to find this lost underwater city. Today, most historians agree that Atlantis is a place of fiction; however, many believe that Plato may have based the island on a real place. While the idea of a sunken city may seem far-fetched, natural occurrences like earthquakes and tsunamis have, in reality, consumed once-thriving civilizations.

A ONCE BUSTLING PORT

One such civilization is the underwater city of Heracleion, also known as Thonis or Thonis-Heracleion. Located near the mouth of the Nile River, Heracleion was an ancient Egyptian port founded around the eighth century B.C., hundreds of years before its famous neighbor, Alexandria. The city served as the main port of entry for Greek ships traveling to Egypt, and also became a city of religious significance due to its large temples devoted to the Egyptian god Amun and his son,

Khonsou. Built on several neighboring islands, Heracleion featured canals and harbors lined with houses and wharfs, all connected by many bridges and ferries.

While Heracleion was a thriving city for centuries, it grew weaker over time as it fell victim to earthquakes, tsunamis, and rising sea levels. By the second century B.C., the main island of the city began eroding due to soil liquefaction. The once hardened ground was inundated with sea water, and gradually the buildings fell into the sea. While a few residents continued living on adjacent islands for several more centuries, by the end of the eighth century A.D., the city of Heracleion had completely disappeared into the Mediterranean Sea.

FROM FORGOTTEN TO FOUND

But the city didn't only vanish from dry land; it also almost vanished from historical memory. Ancient historians and philosophers made note of the city, sometimes working it into mythological chronicles such as the story of Helen of Troy. Hard evidence of its existence, however, was rare and hard to come by. While archeologists discovered several stone slabs inscribed with mentions of Heracleion, they were mostly forgotten, perhaps set aside in favor of researching easier-to-locate Egyptian ruins.

It wasn't until airplanes became commonplace that the ruins of Heracleion were once again seen by human eyes. In 1933, a British Royal Air Force pilot was flying over Abu Qir Bay just east of Alexandria when he spotted the city underwater. Even so, it took until the year 2000 for French underwater archeologist Franck Goddio to reach the ruins, which are located 4.3 miles from the shore, and to begin excavating the city. Goddio helped to set the record straight about the city's name, which, until his discovery, had been assumed to be a separate city from Thonis. But an engraved stele found underwater helped to explain the disparity: Heracleion was the city's Greek name, whereas Thonis was its Egyptian name. Today, most scholars refer to the city as Thonis-Heracleion.

UNDERWATER TREASURE

Clarifying the city's name helped to solve a longstanding archeological puzzle, but Goddio's discovery revealed so much more. A large number of coins, gold jewelry, and pottery were found dating between the sixth and fourth century B.C., leading researchers to conclude that this was the city's most prosperous time. The busy port city enjoyed immense wealth and grandeur during this era, evidenced by its grand temples, intricate architectural details, and bronze statues. Researchers also found more than 70 shipwrecks and 700 ancient ship anchors in the area, a testament to Heracleion's importance as a port city.

Some of the most impressive finds were several nearly intact colossal statues on the sea floor, some more than 16 feet tall and weighing more than five tons. Usually made of red or pink granite, these statues represented Ptolemaic kings and queens, as well as Hapi, the god of the Nile flood. The flooding of the Nile was an annual incident that resulted in fertile soil and good crop conditions, making Hapi an important god of abundance and fertility. The statue was the largest representation of a god ever found in Egypt, indicating Heracleion's dependence on, and appreciation for, the Nile River.

Researchers estimate that only around 5 percent of Heracleion has been excavated, and archeological research continues to this day. The artifacts that have been recovered have been given to the Grand Egyptian Museum in Giza, slated to open in late 2022, so that these amazing finds can be shared with the world. But it is hard not to wonder what sorts of treasures remain buried underwater, patiently waiting to reveal more secrets about the magnificent city consumed by the sea.

NAUCRATIS: GREEK CULTURE IN EGYPT

Located approximately 45 miles southeast of Alexandria, on the western edge of the Nile River delta, the ancient city of Naucratis was the first permanent Greek settlement in Egypt, founded around 570 B.C. While evidence of Greek influence in Egypt dates back to at least 1600 B.C., the two civilizations were at first merely engaged in trading and commerce. But in the seventh century B.C., Greek mercenaries joined the fight of Egyptian pharaoh Apries, who attempted to defeat a former general named Amasis. Although Amasis prevailed and consequently became pharaoh, the new monarch took a liking to the Greeks and allowed them to settle in what would become Naucratis.

The area, once the site of an Egyptian town, soon turned into a major trading port between Greece and Egypt, as well as other Mediterranean civilizations. Greek traders began to settle in the region, and soon Naucratis had a large, prosperous Greek population. The town was a pivotal link between Egypt and the Mediterranean world, and its influence stretched from Phoenicia, Cyprus, and the Levant in the east to Italy in the west. By the time Alexander the Great conquered Egypt in 332 B.C., Naucratis had established itself as a hub of Greek culture, which contentedly coexisted alongside Egyptian society.

Some of the goods exported by Naucratis included wool, textiles, flax, papyrus, perfumes, and *natron*, a sodium-based chemical used during the mummification process. The discovery of such things along trade routes and in the homes of ancient peoples living in the Mediterranean and Aegean regions, has proven to researchers just how influential Naucratis was during its span as a trading port. Evidence suggests that the civilization remained an important city until well into the Byzantine Period of the Roman Empire, but the rise of Alexandria and the shifting Nile eventually led to its downfall. The once-vital civilization faded into obscurity sometime after A.D. 7.

TWO CULTURES, ONE CITY

Fortunately, an English Egyptologist by the name of Flinders Petrie discovered the ruins of Naucratis while excavating the area in 1884, giving archeologists a glimpse into the city's unique mix of Greek and Egyptian culture. The site covers the modern-day villages of Kom-Ge'if, el-Niveria, and el-Niqrash, and, although it has been almost entirely covered by vegetation, researchers have uncovered a large quantity of artifacts. These include Greek-style pottery, stone statuettes, amulets, and large quantities of coins. Archeologists also found evidence of Egyptian-style "tower houses," or tall homes constructed of mud bricks, commonly found along the Nile during the time period.

Remains of sanctuaries dedicated to Greek gods including Castor and Pollux, Hera, Apollo, and Aphrodite were discovered, as well as sanctuaries reserved for Egyptian gods, such as Amun-Ra, Nut, and Khonsu. These findings illustrated the blend of Greek and Egyptian cultures that coexisted in the location.

Scholars estimate that at its height of power, Naucratis had an impressive population of approximately 15,000. This mix of Greek and Egyptian residents not only gave the civilization a distinctive perspective in the ancient world, but it also left an indelible mark on many other civilizations throughout the region. There is no doubt that this Greek city in the middle of Egypt was enormously important during its reign.

PUNT: KINGDOM OF MYTH AND LEGEND

Imagine a kingdom filled with gold, spices, incense, exotic animals, and precious woods. A land so rich with resources that the ancient Egyptians, who already had a reputation for wealth and power, sought out trade with this kingdom to outfit their own temples and rulers. Pharaohs even recorded their travels to this land in inscriptions, drawings, and texts, lauding it as *Ta netjer*, or "the land of the gods."

This "land of the gods" was the Kingdom of Punt, and evidence of its existence dates back to the 25th century B.C., when the Pharaoh Sahure organized the first known expedition to the region. Scholars are unsure of its exact location, but most agree that it was located in northeastern Africa, most probably in the area that is now northern Somalia. Egyptian pharaohs developed fleets of ships to navigate the waters of the Red Sea, creating a trade route between the two kingdoms that lasted for hundreds of years.

FIT FOR A QUEEN

While many Egyptian pharaohs appreciated trade with Punt, the most famous expedition was undertaken in 1493 B.C. by Queen Hatshepsut, the fifth pharaoh of the 18th Dynasty of Egypt. Hatshepsut commissioned artists to record images of the journey, including the inhabitants of the land, the local flora and fauna, and illustrations of King Parahu and Queen Ati, said to be Punt's rulers at the time of the expedition.

Hatshepsut's expedition highlighted some of the extravagant goods Punt supplied to Egypt. In exchange for tools, weapons, metals, and jewelry from Egypt, Punt offered animal skins from leopards, cheetahs, panthers, and giraffes, which were fashioned into clothing for Egyptian priests; spices, incense, aromatic gum, and cosmetics that may have filled Hatshepsut's temples with exotic fragrances; and Punt's gold, which was used for statues, amulets, and other adornments. But perhaps the most impressive items brought back to Egypt were living Boswellia trees, prized for their production of frankincense. These trees marked the first time in recorded history that successful transplants were made of foreign vegetation to a new locale.

TREES TELL THE TALE

It was the trees that Hatshepsut brought back from Punt more than two thousand years ago that gave present-day historians the clues needed to pinpoint the kingdom's ancient location. For decades, scholars debated possible sites, with suggestions ranging from present-day Yemen to the island of Sri Lanka. But Hatshepsut was so impressed with her travels to Punt that she had records of the kingdom inscribed on the walls of her mortuary temple. Thanks to her meticulous record-keeping, archeologists were able to glean information about the mysterious land, including its proximity to water and the animals that were native to the area. This helped to considerably narrow down possible locations, but still left much up for dispute.

Digging deeper, historians discovered that Hatshepsut organized her expedition to Punt specifically to retrieve living frankincense trees. Ancient Egyptians were known to import two kinds of frankincense: a "low" grade and a "high" grade. The low grade was found in the Nile River Valley and could be transported over land. But the high grade was transported by sea, such as occurred with Hatshepsut's expedition.

Records show that 31 of the heavy trees were hand-carried back to her ships, giving researchers a vital clue: the trees could not have been growing very far from shore. A second clue came from the discovery of "high" grade frankincense, obtained from the *Boswellia frereana* tree, in Egyptian tombs. *Boswellia frereana* was only grown close to the seashore in northern Somalia. So, when Egyptians spoke of "high" grade frankincense from the land of Punt, chances are they were referring to present-day Somalia. In fact, the government of Somalia now states in official documentation that the country was once called the "Land of Punt."

MORE TO DISCOVER

Regardless of its exact location, Punt astounded the Egyptians with its affluence, and stories of its many riches and luxuries gave it an air of utopian fable. While inscriptions and ancient texts corroborate its existence, this kingdom filled with gold and riches eventually vanished, leaving behind only stories of its splendor. Sometime after the reign of Ramesses III, the famed kingdom faded from the minds of Egyptians, until it became only a place of myth and legend. But today, many archeologists and historians are bringing the kingdom of Punt back to the forefront, continuing to study the ancient country, its people, and its customs. It's clear that "the land of the gods" has many more stories to tell.

THE SUNKEN CITY OF CANOPUS

Homeric legend tells the story of Menelaus, the king of Sparta, who led the Greek army during the Trojan War. At sea, the king had a ship that was piloted by a handsome young captain named Canopus, who, while visiting the Egyptian coast, was bitten by a poisonous serpent and died. Menelaus built a monument to his ship captain right there on the Egyptian shore, and eventually, a city grew up around it. Referenced by numerous classical scholars, including ancient Greek historian Herodotus and the philosopher Seneca, the city was said to be the ship captain's namesake, Canopus.

Canopus, believed to date back to the 6th century B.C., was said to be an extravagant and decadent city, known for its luxuries. The Roman poet Juvenal noted its "debauchery" in his writings, and the emperor Hadrian was said to have enjoyed a visit to Canopus so much that he built a replica of part of the city at his villa in Tivoli. But the town was also an important religious sanctuary to the gods Osiris and Serapis, and drew pilgrims from all around the region, who believed they could be miraculously healed in the temples there. But the gods were unable to save the city from its eventual demise. Earthquakes, tsunamis, and rising sea levels gradually weakened the land on which Canopus sat, and by the end of the 2nd century B.C., the city sank beneath the waves.

PAST, PRESENT, AND FUTURE

After it succumbed to the sea, the city faded from memory and became, like so many lost civilizations, merely a topic of stories and legends. But in 1933, a Royal Air Force pilot was flying over

Abu Qir Bay on the Mediterranean coast of Egypt when he spotted what looked like ruins beneath the water. The eagle-eyed pilot had discovered not one, but two ancient, submerged cities: the city of Thonis-Heracleion and the city of Canopus.

While excavations of the area around Canopus began in the 1930s, the most significant discoveries have come more recently, under the supervision of French underwater archeologist Franck Goddio. Goddio and his team have found many large architectural elements in the sea, including a 338-foot-long wall that was preserved beneath six feet of sand. The wall is thought to have surrounded a temple, which, if true, would make this Canopus temple the largest ancient Egyptian shrine found in the region.

Also discovered in the area have been limestone blocks, red granite columns, and stones inscribed with hieroglyphs. These stones are of particular interest to archeologists, as they were part of a shrine called the Naos of the Decades, which was dedicated to Shu, the god of the air. Many statue fragments have been found in the area, including a marble head of the god Serapis, and smaller items, like jewelry and coins, hint at the wealth that Canopus once enjoyed.

Researchers believe that only a small percentage of this city beneath the sea has been explored, so there are no doubt many treasures yet to be discovered. In the meantime, Canopus will patiently wait beneath the waves, just as it has for thousands of years.

ASIA AND THE PACIFIC

THE DONG SON

The Dong Son culture, or Dongson, was a late Bronze Age civilization that arose sometime between 1000 and 600 B.C., in what is now the Red River Valley of northern Vietnam. It was best known for its large, ceremonial bronze drums, which could be more than three feet high and weigh up to 220 pounds.

The Dong Son people lived in simple houses with thatched roofs set on stilts, and cultivated rice for food. They also fished and hunted, and raised water buffaloes and pigs. Because they were farmers, they fashioned many types of agricultural tools, including axes, spades and hoes, and created arrowheads and spearheads for fishing and hunting.

Water and seafaring were an important part of Dong Son culture, and some scholars believe that the civilization was a state society that maintained control of the Red River region of Vietnam. Others think that the Dong Son peoples were merely a confederation of villages that shared cultural practices. But either way, evidence of their reverence and respect for the water is clear from their use of "boat burials," or the use of canoe segments in funeral customs. Archeologists have uncovered burial sites in which the deceased was wrapped in a shroud made of vegetable fibers and then placed in a segment of a canoe, with the head at the open end and the feet in the bow of the canoe. Coins, pottery, textiles, and weapons have also been found in Dong Son gravesites.

THE BEAT OF THEIR OWN DRUMS

The most striking and well-known artifacts from the Dong Son culture are their drums, known as Dong Son drums. These were created using a technique called lost-wax casting, in which a metal object is created using a mold of an original object or sculpture. The Dong Son drums were intricately decorated with scenes of daily life, warfare, ritual ceremonies, and geometric patterns, or were created with more simple images of animals, plants, or boats.

The drums were used both for musical instruments, being featured in weddings, festivals, funerals, and other rituals. They were also symbols of power and objects of worship. They were sometimes used for trade as well, with some being found as far away as New Guinea. The Ngoc Lu drum, considered one of the best-preserved examples of a Dong Son drum, is considered one of the national treasures of Vietnam. This drum features three circular concentric panels, decorated with images of animals and people. The outer two panels show figures of deer, egrets, and hornbills, while the innermost panel appears to depict people taking part in a festival. The scene contains illustrations of rice growing and harvesting, but also shows people playing the drums themselves, reinforcing the importance the instrument played in the life of the Dong Son peoples.

The Dong Son culture began to fade sometime around the first century, A.D., but many scholars believe the people of this civilization are the direct descendants of the modern Vietnamese people. The artifacts—and literal national treasures—they left behind continue to remind the people of Vietnam of their ancient past.

THE ACHAEMENID EMPIRE

Founded around 559 B.C., the Achaemenid Empire, also known as the Persian Empire, became the largest empire the world had ever seen. Spanning the Balkan Peninsula in the west to the Indus Valley in the east, the empire covered around 2.1 million square miles and encompassed what are now Iran, Egypt, Turkey, and parts of Afghanistan and Pakistan.

The Achaemenid Empire arose under the leadership of King Cyrus the Great. Before he was known as "great," however, Cyrus was the leader of one of many scattered tribes in Persia, the Pasargadae. The Pasargadae tribe was located near the sprawling but disjointed Median Empire, led by Astyages, Cyrus's grandfather. Despite the family relation, Cyrus laid siege to his grandfather's empire, resulting in many of the Medes revolting against Astyages and joining Cyrus. Cyrus conquered the Median Empire, becoming the Shah, or king, of Persia.

CONQUERED WITH KINDNESS

Cyrus didn't stop with his grandfather's empire; rather, he continued to expand his takeover, next capturing Lydia, a region of western Asia Minor. Lydia's capital, Sardis, was one of the richest cities in the Ionian region, giving Cyrus a quick advantage in his quest for expansion. He then set his sights on Babylon, considered the greatest city in the world at that time. Babylon's king, Nabonidus, was not popular with his people, and Cyrus used that fact to his advantage.

Nabonidus had attempted to quell the religious freedom of the Babylonians, introducing his own religious reform and confiscating religious icons from temples. Cyrus, instead of simply taking Babylon by force, went to the city and performed Babylonian religious rituals that had been suppressed by Nabonidus. He then returned the confiscated idols back to their temples, and told the people that under his rule, they could worship any gods they chose. The citizens of Babylon were enamored by this new leader, and gladly handed him control of the city.

Cyrus became well known for this religious tolerance and embrace of multiculturalism. He was also admired for his mercy, as he never mistreated the cities and kingdoms he conquered. Instead of killing a vanquished king, he would ask for the king's advice and guidance in ruling over a newly acquired city and its subjects. Cyrus the Great even earned praise in the Bible, which tells of his liberation of Hebrew captives in Babylon and his efforts to rebuild Jerusalem.

TAXES AT WORK

When Cyrus died in 530 B.C., he left behind the foundation of a strong kingdom, which saw its greatest height during the rule of Darius I. Darius, who began his reign in 522 B.C., expanded the empire into the Indus Valley, and realized that his vast kingdom needed organization if it were to run smoothly. He divided the empire into 20 provinces known as "satrapies," each of which was run by a "satrap," meaning "protector of the kingdom" or "keeper of the province." The satraps were required to pay a regular tribute to Persia, which was, in effect, a tax.

Darius used this tax to create a navy and to fund public works like irrigation projects, roads, and canals. Darius also designed a postal system, which was not unlike the "Pony Express" that would be used in America thousands of years later. The postal system interconnected the empire using a series of roads which couriers traveled by horseback. The horses would be switched out at predetermined locations to prevent the animals from suffering fatigue. This system was not altogether innocuous, however; Darius used it as a way to keep tabs on each of his satraps, appointing spies to gather information and report back by way of the postal system.

GREAT RICHES, LITTLE HUMILITY

The riches of the Achaemenid Empire grew great, and Darius tasked craftsmen from all over the kingdom to construct an imperial capital at Persepolis. He established a common currency for the empire, and kept large amounts of gold and silver in a large vault in the new capital. Persepolis became a city that showcased the cultures and styles of peoples throughout the kingdom, a vision that the first king, Cyrus, had for the empire.

But Darius lacked much of the humility of Cyrus, seeing himself as exalted beyond his subjects. He eventually dropped the title of "Shah" for the loftier "Shahanshah" ("king of kings"). His arrogance may have led to the unrest that began to plague the empire in 499 B.C., when the Greeks staged a revolt. Darius, seeking to punish the Greeks for their rebellion, sailed a fleet to Athens only to be shockingly defeated. In order to appear strong and in control, Darius raised taxes to rebuild his fleet. But this only led to more unrest and instability, especially in the area of Egypt.

Darius's son, Xerxes, who began his reign in 486 B.C., attempted to quell the discontent in the kingdom, but he proved to be even more arrogant than his father. When the Babylonians began to riot in 482 B.C., Xerxes, who, unlike Cyrus, had no interest in religious or cultural tolerance, sacked the city and tore down a golden statue of Marduk, the Babylonian's patron god. He melted down the gold and kept it for himself, using it to build an army to attack the mutinous Greeks. But the Greeks once again proved victorious, and Xerxes retreated to his wealthy palace to live out his days in luxury and decadence.

THE NEXT "GREAT" RULER

The overconfidence and excesses of the last kings of the Achaemenid Empire no doubt contributed to its downfall. For the next 200 years, the rulers of the kingdom hid in opulent palaces, doing little more than raising taxes, as the once-united empire gradually grew disjointed. The satraps began to grow in power, taking more control of their individual regions. Meanwhile, the huge army of the kingdom, which was once praised for its multiculturalism, became a confused mishmash of troops that spoke different languages and were all trained in different fighting styles. It was only a matter of time before the empire collapsed.

Cyrus the Great had created the world's first known empire, and had paved the way for its prosperity with his ideas of humble governance. Unfortunately, many of his successors saw only a path to power, and their pride led to the end of the kingdom. Someone else was paying attention to the downfall of the Achaemenid Empire: Alexander the Great. Alexander, who had been an enthusiastic admirer of Cyrus the Great, conquered what was left of the Persian Empire in 334 B.C. But unlike the last kings of the Achaemenid Empire, Alexander the Great remembered Cyrus's example and used it as inspiration for his campaigns, swiftly accruing his own infamous empire.

THE CATALHOYUK SETTLEMENT OF ANATOLIA

In 1962, a British archeologist named James Mellaart was accused of smuggling priceless antiquities, supposedly discovered in the Turkish city of Dorak, out of the country. Mellaart claimed to have met a woman who owned many pieces that dated back to ancient Troy, but she would not allow them to be photographed. Instead, Mellaart drew sketches of the items and took notes, later publishing his findings in *The Illustrated London News*. Turkish authorities, however, could find no evidence of the mysterious woman who supposedly showed Mellaart the collection of items, and they concluded that the archeologist fabricated her existence to cover up his own theft. The "Dorak Treasure," as it came to be known, was never found, and Mellaart was barred from reentering Turkey.

This was a shame, as only a few years earlier, in 1958, Mellaart had uncovered the remains of a large settlement near the city of Konya. Mellaart's excavations revealed 18 layers of buildings, suggesting many eras of civilization in the region. The lowest layers dated back to at least 7100 B.C., whereas the top layers dated to 5600 B.C. After Mellaart's involvement in the "Dorak Affair" and his subsequent banishment, this impressive find sat idle for decades.

SETTLING DOWN

It wasn't until 1993 that excavations of the site, known as the Catalhoyuk settlement, began again in earnest. What Mellaart had discovered were the ruins of a town that flourished 9000 years ago and boasted a population of between 8,000 and 10,000 residents. Over time, as the civilization spanned the centuries, there is evidence that the society transitioned from more of a hunter and gatherer lifestyle to one of agriculture and animal husbandry. The city itself is considered an illustration of the progress humans in the Anatolian region achieved when they shifted from nomads to settlers.

Years of modern excavation at the site revealed much about these ancient city-dwellers. One of the most unique aspects of the Catalhoyuk settlement is the arrangement of the houses. There were no roads or paths in the town; rather, the mudbrick houses were constructed in an interconnected style, as if they were a large, human-sized honeycomb. Doors to the houses were located in the rooftops and accessed by ladders, so the roofs themselves served as pathways through the settlement. Large communal ovens were located above the homes, suggesting that the rooftops also served as a gathering place for the residents. Over the centuries, houses were periodically demolished and new houses were built on top of the rubble, leading to a "tell," or a mound, made up of accumulated debris.

EQUALITY AND ART

The Catalhoyuk society was believed to be egalitarian, with men and women holding equal social status. This is evident in the civilization's burial practices, which seem to be relatively similar for everyone within the culture. The dead were tightly wrapped in reed mats and buried right inside the village, often under floors, hearths, or even beds, inside homes. The only exceptions made in burial practices were for children, who were often decorated with beads and colorful ochre, suggesting that children were valued in the society because of a need for help with household labor and a desire for descendants.

But perhaps the most striking feature of the Catalhoyuk settlement is the artwork that the civilization left behind. Nearly every house excavated at the site was found to contain decoration of some sort, including geometric designs and figures of animals, painted directly on to plaster walls. The plaster seems to have been reapplied every season, or even as often as every month, and then drawn on again, suggesting that this art was a central part of the villagers' lives. Many clay figurines of humans and animals have also been found, scattered in garbage pits or buried in floors or walls. Researchers theorize that these figures were used as tokens to ward off bad luck or evil spirits. Even more interesting was the use of animal remains to create artwork. Often the skulls of bulls, with horns prominently pointing into a room, would be mounted into a wall, along with teeth, beaks, and tusks of various other animals.

A NOD TO THE PAST

Some scholars think that the use of these animals in the artwork of the Catalhoyuk settlement was a way of honoring the past, when hunting was vital for survival. Toward the end of its existence, the Catalhoyuk society was much more reliant on domesticated animals and agriculture for sustenance. Archeologists have discovered storage bins that were used for wheat and barley, and the society also grew peas, almonds, pistachios, and fruit near the village. Although hunting continued to be a source of food, it was not as crucial once the civilization began to raise sheep and cattle.

For unknown reasons, the Catalhoyuk settlement was abandoned sometime before the Bronze Age. But the inhabitants left behind a wealth of clues to help us paint a picture of their society. Today, visitors can travel to this UNESCO World Heritage Site, which features a museum and a protected excavation area. Curious history buffs can also view a recreation of a Catalhoyuk house, constructed by archeologists to show what life may have been like in this village 9000 years ago.

THE FAMED ARCH OF CTESIPHON

Believed to be one of the largest cities in the world in the late sixth and early seventh centuries, Ctesiphon was located on the eastern bank of the Tigris River in what is now Iraq. Accounts of Ctesiphon's founding differ, with classical writers often crediting Vardanes I, who was the king of the Parthian Empire from A.D. 40 to 46, with the establishment of the city. The Parthian Empire was a major Iranian political and cultural power between 247 B.C. and A.D. 224, which encompassed the area where Ctesiphon was located.

However, most scholars agree that the city was founded in the late 120s B.C., decades before Vardanes I rose to power. At first, the area was used as a Greek army camp, established by the king Mithridates I, and was located across the river from the Hellenistic city of Seleucia. But in 129 B.C., the Parthian Empire annexed Babylonia, and discovered that Ctesiphon was an ideal city to use as a capital during the winter months.

TWO BECOME ONE

Not only was the winter weather in Ctesiphon ideal for its use as a residence, but its proximity to Seleucia was also a benefit. Seleucia was already a major Mesopotamian city, having been established as the capital of the Seleucid Empire around 305 B.C., and then becoming the western capital of the Parthian Empire in 141 B.C. With a population of around 600,000, Seleucia was a metropolis rivaled only by Rome and Alexandria. Gradually, Ctesiphon and Seleucia merged, becoming what some believe was the largest city in the world at the time.

Its size and location made Ctesiphon a desirable target for outsiders, especially the Roman Empire, which was determined to claim the city as its own. In the span of 100 years, the city was attacked and captured three times: by the emperor Trajan, the Roman general Avidius Cassius, and the emperor Septimius Severus, who also sold thousands of its inhabitants into slavery. The city's palaces were destroyed, and its population was decimated. But in 224, the Parthian Empire came to an end and the Sasanian Empire took its place, resettling Ctesiphon and once again establishing it as a capital city.

A LOFTY ACHIEVEMENT

Under the Sasanian Empire, Ctesiphon flourished and grew even larger. It was during this time that the city constructed the Taq Kasra, also known as the Archway of Ctesiphon. This structure was built as part of the imperial palace complex and featured a remarkable arched hall that measured 121 feet high, 85 feet wide, and 164 feet long. The arch was built without any kind of central framework, requiring builders to use quick-drying cement and to lay the bricks at an angle that would allow them to be supported by the rear wall during construction. The resulting arch was about 22 feet thick at its base, tapering to just over three feet thick at the apex. Until modern construction techniques became the norm, the Taq Kasra arch was the largest manmade free-standing vault in the world.

The massive arch was used as the audience hall for the kings of the Sasanian Empire, until the empire was conquered by the Arabs in A.D. 637. The structure was then used as a mosque for a time, but eventually the Ctesiphon metropolis was abandoned and fell into ruin. When the city of Baghdad, located 22 miles to the northwest of Ctesiphon, was founded in the eighth century, the ruins of the city, including bricks from Taq Kasra, were used to construct the Taj Palace.

CLAIM TO FAME

Fortunately, much of the impressive structure was spared, and today, the Taq Kasra is the only above-ground structure remaining from the ancient city of Ctesiphon. Its massive vault is still considered the largest brick-built arch in the world, and efforts to preserve the landmark have been on-going for many years. Taq Kasra has been the subject of a documentary film, visited by artists, famously photographed by Roald Dahl, and featured on Iraqi postage stamps. Its architecture is so appreciated and loved in its region that it was copied and used for the building that houses the National Museum of Iran in Tehran.

This arch, which is at least 1,400 years old, has faced floods, wars, the threat of terrorist attacks, and the passage of time itself, yet still stands. With restoration efforts underway, there is hope that Taq Kasra will long continue to serve as a reminder of the once-bustling city of Ctesiphon and its 800-year reign as a world metropolis.

DILMUN

Like many of the stories in the Bible, the tale of the Garden of Eden has fascinated readers for centuries. Described as a peaceful paradise full of lush greenery, flowing streams, and trees full of fruit, the garden was the home of Adam and Eve, the first humans ever created. The pair lived there happily until they ate fruit from the one tree God had commanded them to avoid, the tree of the knowledge of good and evil. They were then cast out, never allowed to return.

Some believe the Garden of Eden story is simply a myth, and the description of the plants and streams are the product of an active imagination. Others believe it is true, and, therefore, the garden must have existed at some point in history. Still others settle on a mix of truth and fiction: perhaps the tale isn't entirely true, but maybe it was inspired by a garden that once grew somewhere in the Middle East.

The Bible gives some clues about the location of the famed garden, describing it as the source of water for four rivers it names as the Gihon, Pishon, Tigris, and Euphrates. The Tigris and Euphrates are well known, running from the mountains of Turkey through Syria, and down through Iraq until they drain into the Persian Gulf near Kuwait.

MYTHS AND STORIES

But the unknown locations of the Gihon and Pishon rivers have been debated by scholars for centuries. Some, including Austrian archeologist Eduard Glaser and Latvian-American archeologist Juris Zarins, posit that the Gihon corresponds to the Karun River in Iran, and the Pishon refers to the Wadi Al-Batin river system that runs through Saudi Arabia, Iraq, and Kuwait. If these theories are correct, the Garden of Eden would have been situated at the head of the Persian Gulf, near present-day Kuwait, and right on the edge of an ancient civilization known as Dilmun.

Like the Garden of Eden, Dilmun was once thought to be nothing more than an ancient myth. The mysterious civilization was situated in a land mentioned in Sumerian mythology, where it was believed to be a paradise free of disease and death. Dilmun was filled with divine water sources, which transformed the surrounding dry desert into a garden of greenery, where the gods resided. These included Enki, the god of water, Ninlil, the goddess of wind, and Ninhursag, the mother goddess, who was said to be the caretaker of the plants in the sacred garden.

MASTERS OF THE SEA

But more recently discovered evidence, including ancient Mesopotamian texts that mention Dilmun as an important trading partner and ruins excavated in Bahrain, have made it clear that this civilization was, indeed, very real.

The first mentions of Dilmun date back to Sumerian cuneiform tablets from the third millennium, B.C., but the society was most prosperous during the early centuries of the second millennium. By this time, Dilmun was controlling the trade routes in the Persian Gulf, which was frequently traversed by peoples from Mesopotamia, the Indus Valley, and China.

According to texts that have been found, Dilmun was considered a prosperous land which was filled with many great dwellings. It was said that all of the known countries in the world brought their wares to Dilmun for trade. Dilmun traded precious woods, ivory, gold, and pearls from the gulf in exchange for silver, tin, textiles, olive oil, and grains from their trading partners. They also may have had a monopoly on copper, which was mined in the area of modern Oman and distributed to Mesopotamian cities.

Sometime after 1720 B.C., Dilmun began to decline in influence. By 1500 B.C., foreign powers began to take over the civilization, including Mesopotamia, Babylonia, and Assyria. Dilmun also suffered from the effects of increasing piracy in the Persian Gulf, which interrupted their trading routes. After the collapse of Babylon in 538 B.C., the name "Dilmun" was no longer even used in texts. The civilization lapsed into obscurity, relegated only to the myths and stories that were told about its existence.

UNCOVERING EVIDENCE

For centuries, the ancient Sumerian writings were the only evidence known to prove the existence of the Dilmun civilization. But in the 1950s, archeologists began to excavate a mound created from the rubble of different settlements on a single site, on the island country of Bahrain. The newest layer dated to the 18th century, when a Portuguese fort was built on the site. The Arabic word for "fort," *qal'at*, gives the location its name, Qal'at al-Bahrain. But it is the lowest layers of the tell, which date back to 2300 B.C., that have given the location its reputation as Bahrain's "most important site in antiquity."

This site, which is situated on a Persian Gulf port, is believed to have been the capital of the Dilmun civilization. Three consecutive Dilmun cities are found within the tell, one on top of the other. Evidence of ancient trade, such as ivory and copper artifacts, have been uncovered, as well as burial grounds, Dilmun stamp seals, the remains of houses and streets, and large warehouses, which hint at Dilmun's prosperous economy. Nearby are carved stones marking the entrance of a chamber with an altar inside, and the presence of blackened animal bones and charred earth suggests that sacrifices to the gods were once performed in the location.

And the ruins at Qal'at at-Bahrain aren't the only evidence of Dilmun that has been discovered in recent years. In the nearby town of Saar, even more ancient remains have been found. The ruins in this area include residential dwellings and a cemetery, which is laid out in a honeycomb pattern. Archeologists have even found what they believe are the remnants of restaurants and shops, suggesting that this region of Dilmun was quite a thriving city.

THE TWO SEAS

While Dilmun is believed to have encompassed eastern Saudi Arabia and Kuwait as well as Bahrain, it seems clear that the tiny island nation was important to the entire civilization. At just under 300 square miles, the tiny country of Bahrain is the smallest Arab nation and the third smallest country in Asia. Its name is said to mean "two seas," but the "seas" it refers to are unclear. Some scholars believe it is in reference to the bay on the east and west of the island, or the seas to the north and south.

But perhaps the more likely meaning has to do with the two types of water naturally found on and around the island—saltwater and freshwater. Until modern days, when the population of Bahrain began to outgrow the resources, the island had an abundance of underground freshwater springs. For an island that receives barely more than three inches of rain a year, these springs were vital to the growth of the region. To ancient peoples, the sight of fresh, life-giving water bubbling up from the ground of an island surrounded by undrinkable saltwater must have seemed like a gift from the gods.

And that's exactly how the people of Dilmun described their land, as a fertile paradise fit for the gods. A Sumerian poem, featuring the gods Enki and Ninhursag, extols Dilmun as "pure," "pristine," and full of "fresh waters."

Whether or not this ancient land was the inspiration, or location, of the Garden of Eden may never be known for certain. But the myths and stories of the enigmatic Dilmun will no doubt continue to fascinate for generations to come.

GOBEKLI TEPE

Ask any archeology buff or history lover to name a megalithic stone monument, and the name Stonehenge will frequently come up. And for good reason: This ring of 13-foot-high, 7-foot-wide stones, each weighing around 25 tons, was built sometime between 3000 and 2000 B.C., using construction methods that are still unknown. Somehow, without the benefit of modern technology, humans were able to create an impressive memorial made of massive monoliths that continues to stand on the Salisbury Plain in Wiltshire, England, thousands of years after its creation.

Stonehenge may be several millennia old, but it is not the oldest known megalithic monument in the world. That honor belongs to the structures of Gobekli Tepe, an archeological site near the town of Urfa in Turkey. In this dry, rocky area of southeastern Anatolia, structures dating to between 9500 and 8000 B.C.—or approximately 6000 years prior to Stonehenge—have been uncovered.

POTBELLY HILL

While the site was noted in an archeological survey in 1963, it was at first believed to be nothing more than an abandoned medieval cemetery. Its true significance was originally recognized by German archeologist Klaus Schmidt, who began excavations of the region in 1995. To Schmidt, it was obvious that the 50-foot-high rounded hill, which is surrounded by lower hills and flat plateaus, was a man-made feature. This rounded curve of the landscape was dubbed Gobekli Tepe ("potbelly hill" in English).

Schmidt immediately located megaliths buried close to the surface of the hill, and further excavation revealed some impressive discoveries. Several circular structures are located at the site, each laid out with two large stone pillars in the center, some up to 16 feet tall, surrounded by a circle of smaller stones. The circular structures vary in size, with the largest being 65 feet across. While some of the stones are bare, others have been intricately carved with images of animals including foxes, lions, snakes, and vultures. Other stones, especially the larger pillars, have anthropomorphic qualities, having been carved with human features such as arms, hands, and clothing. Excavations have also uncovered animal bones, which suggest the area was used for ritual sacrifices as well as celebratory feasts.

What Schmidt did not find, however, was any evidence of a human settlement, such as houses, cooking hearths, or trash pits. The collection of circular structures, ritualistic carvings, bone fragments, and lack of evidence to show that humans ever permanently inhabited the location led Schmidt to name Gobekli Tepe "the world's first temple."

PREHISTORIC PARADISE

Located on the edge of the "Fertile Crescent," an area of mild climate and land suitable for cultivation that stretches through the Middle East from the Persian Gulf to the Mediterranean Sea, the dry, brown land would have looked much different

11,000 years ago when the structures of Gobekli Tepe were being built. Rivers ran across the land, inviting flocks of birds and herds of gazelle to the flowing water. Fruit and nut trees, as well as fields of wild barley and wheat, grew throughout the region, providing food for the hunter-gatherer tribes who migrated from Africa and the Levant.

In fact, Schmidt believed that the area would have seemed like a paradise to prehistoric peoples, perhaps inspiring them to create a place of worship in the midst of the natural beauty. This "cathedral on a hill," as he called it, attracted pilgrims in the surrounding area, from up to 90 miles away, who followed similar shamanic practices. There is also evidence that Gobekli Tepe may have been created as a way to venerate the dead, and human graves will one day be uncovered at the site.

But what has already been uncovered is quite remarkable. The megalithic structures of Gobekli Tepe were built before the discovery of metal, the creation of pottery, or the invention of writing. Yet the large amount of tools found at the site, including knives and chopping implements made of flint, are a testament to the peoples' determination to build their "temple." With these simple tools, stonecutters would have been able to chip away at the surrounding area's limestone to carve out huge pillars. Somehow, they then managed to transport the pillars, weighing up to 16 tons, to the sites of the monuments and arrange them in circles.

WHICH CAME FIRST: COMMUNITY OR TEMPLE?

Around 15,000 different animal bones have been found, the majority of which are from gazelle. But researchers have also found wild boar, deer, wild sheep, ducks, and geese. None of the animal bones found have been from domesticated animals, which suggests that animal husbandry and domestication had not yet occurred. However, the presence of sheep and different types of wild grain provided the creators of Gobekli Tepe with everything they needed to transition from hunter-gatherers to settled farmers. And there is evidence in nearby locations that this is precisely what happened within 1,000 years of the construction of Gobekli Tepe.

But before humans began to construct permanent settlements and learned to cultivate crops, Schmidt believed that they created religious practices and temples for worship. Before uncovering the ruins of Gobekli Tepe, it was assumed that humans never built religious sites before they were settled and felt secure in their resources. However, the discovery of "the world's first temple" forced researchers to rethink this theory. It may, in fact, have been the other way around: Perhaps working together on the construction of huge megalithic monuments created a sense of community that eventually led to a permanent settlement. After all, such a substantial undertaking would require quite a large population of workers, who would all need food and shelter as they worked on their massive project.

UNKNOWN PURPOSE

Whether civilization rose before or after the creation of Gobekli
Tepe is still up for debate. While Schmidt, who died in 2014,
was convinced that the area covers a burial ground for a cult of
the dead, other archeologists have different theories. Considering the site was built 11,000 years ago, at a time when humans
were concerned with issues unique to the era and possessed
different interpretations of many aspects of life, it is impossible
to know what the builders had in mind when they created
their structures. Some believe that the large number of "men-
acing" animals carved into the pillars—like lions, snakes, and
scorpions—as opposed to tame creatures like deer or sheep,
suggests that those who carved the stones were attempting
to assuage their fears of nature. Or perhaps the fierce creatures
were meant to be totems to ward off evil spirits or bad luck.

Others think Schmidt was on the right track, pointing to the
many carvings of vultures, which many societies have believed
carry the flesh of the dead to the heavens, on the stone pillars.
Some researchers even think that excavations will one day reveal
evidence that humans did, in fact, settle permanently at Gobekli
Tepe. Since only about five percent of the area has been uncovered, it would seem that this is a definite possibility.

MONOLITHIC MYSTERIES

Gobekli Tepe has presented archeologists with one more
mystery, as well. The rings of monoliths were not all built
at the same time; rather, when one was completed, it was

deliberately covered up with dirt and another ring would be constructed, either nearby or right on top of the old one. What's more, when the site began to lose relevance to ancient peoples sometime around the eighth century B.C., they did not simply abandon the structures—they buried them. What was the significance of deliberately burying monuments that required so much effort to construct? As with so many other of the site's enigmas, the answer is unclear.

With thousands of years separating modern humans from the builders of Gobekli Tepe, it is likely that we'll never know all the answers to the questions the monuments pose. But their discovery has forced us to question much of what we thought we knew about ancient peoples, religious practices, and the rise of civilization. As more and more of the site is excavated, perhaps we'll be surprised, confused, or amazed by what we find. And for anyone who loves history, the questions and puzzles uncovered will be welcome revelations.

THE HIDDEN IRAQI TREASURE OF LAGASH

In 1887, German archeologist Robert Koldewey, famous for his excavations of Babylon, began excavating a large archeological mound in what is now Iraq. Koldewey spent only six weeks exploring the large site, which was about 20 feet high and measured approximately two miles by one mile, and he couldn't be certain what he had uncovered. It wasn't until new excavations began in 1953 that researchers realized that Koldewey had discovered the remains of Lagash, an ancient Mesopotamian city state.

Dating back to the third millennium B.C., Lagash, which is located near the junction of the Tigris and Euphrates rivers, was actually much larger than its first excavators realized. The city state encompassed the ancient cities of Girsu, Nina, Uruazagga, Erim, and many others, and at its height spanned an area of about 620 square miles. It was ruled by independent kings, the first being Ur-Nanshe, who rose to power around 2550 B.C. But the kingdom truly flourished under the ruler Gudea, who reigned from approximately 2144 to 2124 B.C.

KING GUDEA

Gudea engaged in trade with other kingdoms, including Syria and Arabia, to procure wood, stone, copper, and gold for the construction of many temples and other structures. He was also known for placing many statues of himself, approximately 27 in total, in temples throughout the kingdom. These statues were created with such great detail and craftsmanship that we have a rather good idea of what Gudea looked like, even though he lived long before photography was invented or even painted portraits became commonplace.

In addition to establishing trade with far-off lands, Gudea constructed many irrigation channels, encouraged artistic development, cancelled the debts of many of his people, and allowed women to own land. Under his rule, Lagash continued to grow until it contained 17 large cities, eight district capitals, and more than 40 smaller villages. Some scholars believe that from 2075 to 2030 B.C., Lagash was the largest city in the world.

PRICELESS FINDS, HIDDEN RUINS

By 1980, only around five percent of the region around Lagash had been excavated, and work was forced to stop during the Iran-Iraq War that spanned from 1980 to 1988. Sporadic excavations resumed in 1990, but have often been plagued by looters, who are not only aware of the archeological significance of the site, but know that security in the region is lacking. Still, plenty of ancient artifacts have been uncovered, including 30,000 mud slabs with cuneiform writing, numerous vases, and stone carvings.

Around 50 temples have been identified at the site, although many remain buried beneath the brown hills that dot the area. But several complexes have been excavated, revealing large structures that would have been used for the worship of deities as well as for celebrations and festivals. Some temple complexes have dozens of rooms inside, and many were constructed with large courtyards in the middle. Along with the temples, several structures believed to be kitchens have been found, complete with ovens, storage vats, and pottery. In one such structure, a tablet with the words "the brewery" were found, suggesting a very modern kind of specialization.

Because of ongoing conflicts in Iraq, and the safety issues that go along with them, the excavation of Lagash has been slow-going. Iraqi archeologists are eager to raise awareness of their challenges, in the hopes that researchers from all over the world will take an interest in the ancient treasures that remain to be discovered in Lagash.

THE JEWEL OF THE MONGOL EMPIRE: KARAKORUM

The Mongol Empire was the largest contiguous empire in the history of the world. At its height, it reigned from the Sea of Japan all the way to eastern Europe, covering more than 17 percent of the land on Earth. The empire is probably best known for its original leader, Genghis Khan, who united the nomadic tribes of East Asia before setting out to expand his rule in all directions.

In 1220, the Khan chose a small village called Karakorum, located in what is now northwestern Mongolia, as his base of operations for an invasion of China. Aside from being the Khan's headquarters, the town remained relatively inconsequential until the Mongol conquest of the Jin Dynasty in 1234. Genghis Khan himself died in 1227, but after the defeat of the Jin empire his son, Ögedei, began to construct walls around Karakorum and ordered a palace be built.

A QUICKLY GROWING CITY

Karakorum's location, on a well-traveled east to west trading route on what is now known as the Silk Road, was considered ideal to serve as the capital of the rapidly expanding Mongol Empire. The rectangular walls built by Ögedei measured approximately one mile by one and a half miles and enclosed brick buildings, a dozen shamanistic shrines, mosques, and the palace, which featured 64 wooden columns standing on granite bases.

Ögedei and his successors continued to enlarge and build upon Karakorum, until it became a central location for world politics. At times, especially when the Khan's court was present, the population of the town would grow to such an extent that temporary yurts would be raised just outside the city to accommodate everyone. Merchants and craftsmen sold their wares in the city center, while traders frequently passed through with merchandise from far-off locations.

The city was known for its metallurgy, and produced an abundance of iron cauldrons, metal ornaments, axel rings for horse-drawn carts, and arrowheads. Artisans created glass beads for jewelry and cloth from the wool they gathered from their flocks of sheep. Rich silks from China made their way to the city through trade, and were highly prized by the Mongol elites.

THE STUNNING SILVER TREE

To the Khan and his court, Karakorum was an extraordinary city that deserved an extraordinary centerpiece for its palace courtyard, and Parisian goldsmith Guillaume Bouchier was asked to carry out the task. Bouchier created a large tree sculpted of silver and other precious metals, with branches extending over and into the palace. Four golden serpents wound their way around the trunk, and a trumpet angel stood atop the tree. The serpents and angel were automatons—moving machines with control mechanisms—that must have stunned the 13th century crowds who gathered in the palace courtyard to watch. At the Khan's word, the angel would raise the trumpet to its lips and the four serpents would pour beverages from their mouths into a large silver basin at the base of the tree. The Silver Tree of Karakorum, as it was called, delighted the palace's guests.

Sadly, the magnificent Silver Tree of Karakorum, and much of the city itself, were razed in the late 1300s as the Ming Dynasty arose. Much of what we know today about Karakorum comes from the detailed account of a Flemish Franciscan missionary named Friar William of Rubruck. The friar described a cosmopolitan, religiously tolerant, and multicultural city. But he also spoke of the "arrogance" of the Mongols, who assumed William had come to barter for peace and an alliance on behalf of King Louis IX. Many of the people he met in Karakorum had been captured by the Mongols during raids on their lands, including the talented goldsmith, Guillaume Bouchier.

DISCOVERY AND EXCAVATION

For centuries after the city was razed, its location was unclear; but the Erdene Zuu Monastery, the oldest monastery in Mongolia, provided clues. This Buddhist monastery was built using stones from the ruins of Karakorum, but this fact didn't quite click in the minds of archeologists until 1889. In that year, Serbian archeologist Nikolai Yadrintsev discovered that the monastery did, indeed, stand directly adjacent to the Mongol capital.

Excavations of Karakorum began in earnest in 1933, revealing paved roads, brick buildings, kilns, and evidence of metalwork. The kilns were of particular interest to researchers, who concluded that the Mongols used them to produce ceramic roof tiles, tableware, sculptures, and, most impressively, water pipes. There is even evidence that the Mongols created heated floor systems as well as "bed-stoves," traditional heated platforms used in cold weather for both sleeping and for general activities during the day.

Although the Mongol capital was eventually moved from Karakorum to Khanbaliq—today known as Beijing, the capital of the People's Republic of China—the city remained a symbol of Genghis Khan's power for centuries. Referring to his first impression of Karakorum and its people, William of Rubruck wrote, "When I found myself among them, it seemed to me of a truth that I had been transported into another world." It is a shame that this "world," at one time impressive, grand, and magnificent, has been lost to time.

THE KHMER EMPIRE

Just north of the resort town of Siem Reap in Cambodia lies the sprawling Angkor Wat temple. Built in the early 12th century, the temple was constructed to honor the Hindu god Vishnu, but later became a Buddhist site. It is still considered an important pilgrimage destination for Buddhists, and is believed to be the largest religious monument in the world. The temple is even prominently featured on Cambodia's national flag, a testament to the importance this structure holds in the hearts and minds of its people.

Angkor Wat is, no doubt, the most lasting symbol of the Khmer Empire of Southeast Asia, which lasted from the 9th to the 15th centuries. The empire was formed by the Khmer people, who, by the seventh century, inhabited much of the area along the Mekong River. Many kingdoms in the area often warred against each other, until a man named Jayavarman II set out to conquer these fighting factions. He successfully managed to overcome and unite a series of territories, and, once his victories were complete, declared himself *Chakravartin*, meaning "universal ruler."

PEACE, WAR, AND TEMPLES

Jayavarman II began his rule in A.D. 802, which is the date used to mark the beginning of the Khmer Empire, and reigned for 33 years. He and his successors expanded the empire without the use of violence and engaged in the trade of goods and services with nearby regions. The king Yasovarman I established the capital of the empire at Yasodharapura—also known as Angkor.

Over the next few centuries, the Khmer empire expanded, but their peaceful beginnings were soon marred by wars and conflicts. The kingdom annexed lands to the west and north, but the Vietnamese and the Cham peoples (located in what is today central Vietnam), proved to be fierce fighters who refused to allow their lands to be taken by the Khmer. As a result, although the Khmer empire eventually covered most of what is today Myanmar, Thailand, Laos, Cambodia, and part of southern China, it was never able to annex the bulk of Vietnam.

But the inability to attain this area was of little consequence to the mighty Khmer empire. The people of the kingdom were prolific builders, creating not just temples and monuments, but a network of infrastructure including roads, bridges, canals, and reservoirs. The main highway constructed by the Khmers was almost 500 miles long. King Jayavarman VII, who ruled from 1181 to 1215, is credited with building more than 100 hospitals and establishing what could be considered the world's first known healthcare system.

THE GREAT CITY

Along with Angkor Wat, which was built between 1122 and 1150, the Khmers constructed Banteay Srei, a temple prized for its intricate carvings, and Ta Keo, the first temple to be built entirely of sandstone, in addition to many other impressive structures. In the late 12th century, Jayavarman VII established Angkor Thom, meaning "great city," as the capital of the Khmer empire, with his own temple, Bayon, located at the center. This complex was built inside Angkor as a "city within a city," and at the height of the Khmer empire, Angkor was the largest pre-industrial urban center in the world. The city covered an area about the size of Los Angeles, and researchers estimate that its population may have topped one million.

During this time, the Khmer people enjoyed wealth and prosperity, engaging in festivals and celebrations year-round. Horse races, music, dancing, fireworks, and other entertainment were part of their culture. They relied heavily on rice farming, fishing, and other agriculture for their economy, selling their wares in open-air marketplaces. Interestingly, most of the trade and commerce in the empire was run by women, who were respected for their abilities in these matters. Society was ordered according to the Hindu caste system, until Buddhism eclipsed Hinduism as the most popular religion in the region in the 13th century.

RISE OF THE SUKHOTHAI AND DOWNFALL OF THE KHMER

Scholars are unsure of why the Khmer empire began to steadily decline after the 13th century, although some propose the switch to Buddhism may have contributed to the change in political and social systems. Others suggest a breakdown in infrastructure or even a plague may have affected the kingdom to the point of collapse. But the most likely reason for the downfall of the empire is a great migration of Thai peoples from the north of the kingdom.

In 1238, many of these peoples, living in the Lavo kingdom, a state within the Khmer empire, revolted and gained independence. They chose the city of Sukhothai as their capital, and became known as the Sukothai kingdom, encompassing much of modern-day Thailand. Other Thai migrants began annexing regions for themselves, and in 1431, the kingdom of Ayutthaya took Angkor, driving out the last king of the Khmer empire, Ponhea Yat.

Today, visitors flock to Angkor to see the city's monuments and temples, which, until the 19th century, had been largely hidden by the surrounding forest. Dozens of archeological sites have been uncovered, restored, and preserved, and the tourism they attract is vital to Cambodia's economy. The intricate structures serve as a legacy left behind by the once great Khmer empire.

THE LAPITA: CULTURE OF THE SOUTH PACIFIC

When American archeologists Edward W. Gifford and Richard Shulter Jr. began excavating a site in New Caledonia, an archipelago in the South Pacific, in 1952, they heard the locals using the word *xapeta'a*, which means "to dig a hole" or "the place where one digs" in the Haveke language. But the researchers misheard the word, and from their confusion they coined the name "Lapita," using it to name the civilization they'd uncovered on Grande Terre, the largest of the islands in New Caledonia.

Gifford and Shulter discovered pottery fragments that were dated to around 800 B.C., and which spoke to the ancient travels of a seafaring people. The Lapita are believed to have originated in the northern Philippines and nearby islands, and began migrating to the islands of the South Pacific Ocean around 1600 B.C., becoming the first people to colonize the area. Evidence of their existence has been found at more than 200 sites, not only in New Caledonia, but also in New Guinea, Fiji, Tonga, Samoa, and the Solomon Islands. Many researchers believe the Lapita peoples made it to New Zealand, as well, and some even suggest they traveled as far as South America.

SAILING AND SETTLING

It is astounding to think that people who lived thousands of years before cruise liners and airplanes were able to traverse a vast ocean to find new lands, yet that is exactly what the Lapita peoples accomplished. Sadly, there is little evidence to shine a light on how they traveled such long distances by sea, but the civilization must have possessed an impressive amount of navigational knowledge. They are believed to have been skilled sailors, who understood exactly how to use the wind to their advantage, and who used indications like the sun and stars, shadows, and the flight of birds as guides to keep them on course.

Regardless of how they accomplished their exploration of the Pacific, the Lapita left behind artifacts and evidence that give us a glimpse into their lives. The Lapita grew taro, coconuts, yams, bananas, and breadfruit, and supplemented their diet by fishing off the islands where they settled. This was an easy feat, since most of their villages were located on the shoreline, rather than further inland. Researchers theorize this may have been to avoid disease-carrying insects, such as mosquitoes, or perhaps because areas inland were already occupied by other civilizations. This is not to say they avoided inland locations altogether, however; in the Bismarck Archipelago, a group of islands off the coast of New Guinea, most of the Lapita settlements were inland. These villages were located near sources of obsidian, which the Lapita used to create tools and as a commodity for trading with other cultures.

A FACE FROM THE PAST

The burial practices of the Lapita were particularly interesting, demonstrating that the culture went to great lengths to honor their dead. Most people were buried on their back, but some were interred on their stomachs. Others were in what researchers call "yoga positions," with legs bent in different ways. Special pottery, used only in burials, was often included in the gravesites. But the most unusual aspect of Lapita burials was the removal of the skulls after body decomposition. The skulls were then placed in ceramic pots and used for ceremonial purposes. The removal of skulls was a known practice to archeologists amongst the peoples of the Pacific, but many researchers believe the custom may have originated with the Lapita.

While this practice was common, it was not always carried out. In fact, in 2002, a complete Lapita skeleton caused quite a stir in the archeological world. Discovered in central Fiji, the female skeleton was found in a settlement dating back to 1000 B.C., buried in five feet of beach sand and surrounded by Lapita pottery. The woman's skull was remarkably well-preserved, and researchers were able to create a computer model of it, which they then used to create a representation of the woman's face. She was dubbed Mana, a word that means "truth" in the Lau dialect of Malaita, the most populous island of the Solomon Islands. Mana became the first depiction of a Lapita person the world had ever seen. She has since been laid to rest in the same area of Fiji where she was discovered.

While the Lapita culture may have faded away around 500 B.C., the ancestors of this civilization are very much alive today in the people of Polynesia, Micronesia, and Melanesia. Some even believe that the modern tattoos favored by the people of Oceania are based on motifs used in Lapita pottery. The people in these regions work to keep their traditions and spiritual values alive, ensuring that the customs that began with the Lapita will never truly disappear.

Birthplace of Buddha

According to legend, sometime around 563 B.C. a pregnant queen named Mayadevi, who lived in what is today Nepal, was traveling when she stopped in a beautiful flower garden. Under a sal tree, she gave birth to a son, who was named Siddhartha Gautama. Thirty-five years later, Prince Siddhartha became Gautama Buddha, the founder of Buddhism, teaching devotees the path to enlightenment and Nirvana.

Today, the location of the garden where Buddha is believed to have been born is known as Lumbini, and it is one of the holiest sites for followers of the religion. Located in the Rupandehi District of the Lumbini Province in Nepal, the region is situated very close to the Indian border. While it was known to be a pilgrimage destination for Buddhist followers for centuries after Prince Siddhartha was born, as Hinduism and Islam made their way into the country by the 8th century, A.D., Lumbini was neglected and eventually forgotten.

THE ASHOKA PILLAR

But a great benefactor of Buddhism, Ashoka the Great, emperor of the Maurya Empire, had formally declared in 249 B.C. that Lumbini was the birthplace of the Buddha. To commemorate the site, the emperor created an inscribed stone pillar so that future visitors would understand the significance of the location. Over time, the pillar was damaged, as documented by a Chinese Buddhist monk named Xuanzang, who made a pilgrimage to the site in the 7th century. Xuanzang noted a pillar, topped by a sculpture of a horse, that was split in two and lying on the ground.

After Lumbini's popularity waned in an increasingly Hindu and Islamic area, the pillar was also forgotten, much of it buried and hidden underground. Then, in 1869, German archeologist Alois Anton Führer, who specialized in the study of South Asian cultures, began excavating the Ashoka pillar, which had been discovered several years earlier. As Führer dug away the earth that had concealed the pillar for so long, he found something that the monk Xuanzang had not mentioned in the record of his travels: the inscription that Ashoka the Great had added to the stone pillar, marking the location of the Buddha's birth.

REDISCOVERY

Although Führer was later found to have faked some of his archeological discoveries and was forced to end his career in disgrace, most scholars agree that the pillar of Ashoka is indeed authentic. Regardless, the discovery served to reignite interest in the "lost" city of Lumbini, and placed the sacred location back on the map. Indian archeologist Purna Chandra Mukherjee took over the excavations of the area after Führer's misdeeds. Many modern researchers credit Mukherjee with truly "discovering" Lumbini, as he engaged in careful, methodical work in the area, uncovering ancient monasteries, temples, and sculptures.

Along with the ruins of ancient monasteries, researchers have found an ancient bathing pond and a bodhi tree, which, according to legend, is the same type of tree under which Buddha attained enlightenment in 500 B.C. In the 1930s, the governor of the region ordered restoration projects at Lumbini, in order to make the destination more attractive to tourists. But the projects also resulted in the loss of some of the ancient artifacts, prompting the Nepalese Department of Archeology to take control of the site. It was later protected under the Ancient Monument Preservation Act of 1956.

AN ENLIGHTENED DESTINATION

Modern Lumbini, which is three miles long and one mile wide, is divided into three sections: the Sacred Garden, the Monastic Zone, and the Cultural Center and New Lumbini Village. The Monastic Zone contains monasteries and schools that represent the Theravada, Mahayana, and Vajrayana Buddhist traditions. The Cultural Center and New Lumbini Village is where visitors will find a museum, shops, research institute, administrative buildings, and the Lumbini Crane Sanctuary, which helps to protect sarus cranes and preserve the natural ecosystem of the area.

But the heart of Lumbini is the Sacred Garden, where the site of Buddha's birth has been marked with a stone. The area also features the Mayadevi Temple, the Ashoka Pillar, and a pond where Mayadevi was said to have ritually bathed before giving birth to the Buddha. The area is popular not only with followers of Buddhism, but with anyone seeking peaceful reflection or quiet meditation.

Modern Lumbini has been designed to mirror the spiritual path of Buddhism. The first area that greets visitors is the Cultural Center and New Lumbini Village, a busy area of "worldly activities." From there, visitors leave the distractions behind and journey to the Monastic Zone, representative of learning more about Buddhism and its traditions. Finally, the quiet enlightenment of the Sacred Garden awaits, where guests can reflect on their own spiritual paths. For tourists from around the world, Lumbini is not just an archeological site full of ancient artifacts, it is also a journey unto itself.

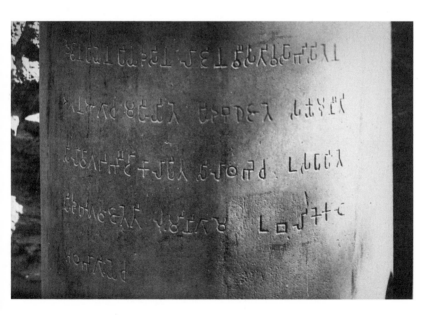

THE DEMISE OF MOHENJO-DARO

Located west of the Indus River in the Sindh province of Pakistan, the ancient city of Mohenjo-Daro is notable for its advanced infrastructure, which was unusually complex for its time. While the people who lived here seemed to possess greater knowledge and resources than their ancient counterparts, they abandoned their great city for unknown reasons, leaving behind some chilling clues.

AN AMAZING FIND

As early as the 1850s, British colonial officials discovered bricks belonging to the Mohenjo-Daro site, but they were unaware of their importance. It was not until 1920, when an Indian archeologist by the name of R.D. Banerji visited the area, that the site was discovered. Banerji was excavating what he believed to be a Buddhist stupa—a mound-like structure used as a place of meditation—when he stumbled upon artifacts made of flint. Further excavation revealed an impressive Bronze-Age city. The city, thought to have been established around 2500 B.C., exhibited an impressive and advanced level of city planning, with a grid-like layout, a sewer system, and houses with bathrooms and toilets. Even the bricks used to build the city, once thought to be insignificant, were found to be more well-constructed than other bricks of the age.

Other finds included carved figures, copper and stone tools, metal bowls and pots, jewelry, and toys. Archeologists also discovered tablets with writing in the Indus Script, but this language has never been fully deciphered, leaving researchers to glean what information they could about this civilization from the other discoveries at the site. Even so, it was clear that the inhabitants of this city were advanced for their time. Although its original name is unknown, archeologists dubbed the city Mohenjo-Daro, which is often interpreted to mean "mound of the dead."

THE MYSTERY OF THE 44

Much of Mohenjo-Daro had the appearance of a city abandoned. But in the uppermost levels of the city, researchers made a chilling discovery: 44 human skeletons, scattered throughout streets and houses, buried under layers of rubble, ash, and debris. The bodies were contorted into strange and unnatural positions. Some of the people appeared to have died while attempting to crawl to safety, which led archeologists to immediately assume that these 44 people had died a violent death. Had the city been attacked by an enemy? Some believed that an armed band of Indo-Aryans, a nomadic tribe from the northwest, ambushed the city as the 44 attempted to defend it. However, no weapons were found near the bodies, and none showed evidence of violent injuries.

Others believed that the bodies' contorted appearance was not due to violence, but rather illness. Cholera outbreaks were common at the time, and evidence seems to suggest that Mohenjo-Daro was prone to flooding. Even with their advanced sewer systems, a flood easily could have resulted in an outbreak in the city. But even this theory is not well-accepted, as modern scientific dating techniques have shown that these 44 people did not die at the same time. Some died years—and perhaps even centuries—earlier than others. Most scientists now conclude that the 44 probably died of natural causes.

THE MYSTERY DEEPENS

Even if the 44 skeletons found at Mohenjo-Daro are the result of natural deaths, questions remain. Why, in a city so obviously advanced and orderly, were these people's bodies left so unceremoniously and haphazardly? To archeologists, it appears as if the 44 were simply "dumped" into hastily-dug graves. Why have no other cemeteries or burial sites ever been found within the city? Estimates put the population of Mohenjo-Daro at around 40,000; surely these 44 were not the only people who died while the city existed.

But perhaps the most perplexing question is also the most basic: Why did the thousands of inhabitants of Mohenjo-Daro abandon their sophisticated city? With only an indecipherable language and few clues to go on, we may never know.

MAGICAL NAN MADOL

Pohnpei is the largest of the Senyavin Islands, which belong to the Pohnpei State in the Federated States of Micronesia. But at only 129-square-miles and with a population of just over 36,000, this "large" island is quite small, occupying less space than the Hawaiian island of Lanai. But one of the most significant features of this area is found on an even tinier island off the coast of Pohnpei known as Temwen. Here, sitting on a coral reef in a lagoon, are the ruins of Nan Madol.

This city was once the capital of the Saudeleur Dynasty, the first government to unite the people of Pohnpei, who had been disorganized and lawless after they first settled on the island. According to legend, the dynasty was established around A.D. 1100 by twin brothers, Olisihpa and Olosohpa, who were said to be sorcerers. They arrived at the island in a large canoe from a mythical place known as Western Katau and built an altar on Temwen Island to worship Nahnisohn Sahpw, the god of agriculture. After Olisihpa died, Olosohpa appointed himself king and married a local woman, siring twelve generations of Saudeleur rulers. This not-very-reliable legend also claims that when the brothers built their altar on Temwen, they magically levitated rocks with the aid of a flying dragon.

CITY ON THE REEF

Unfortunately, the real story of how the Saudeleur Dynasty originated is unknown, but researchers do believe that part of the legend is true. While they were certainly not sorcerers or magicians, the people who built the structures on Temwen were most likely a foreign tribe who migrated to Pohnpei. After they arrived, they chose a leader, known as the Saudeleur, who ruled from Nan Madol and managed to unite the tumultuous peoples of Pohnpei.

Nan Madol is the only known ancient city built atop a coral reef, and is made up of more than 90 artificial islands. Tidal canals and waterways crisscross the city, giving it its nickname, "the Venice of the Pacific." In fact, "Nan Madol" can be roughly translated to "within the intervals," in reference to the winding watery pathways that provide a method of transportation through the city. Buildings in the city were constructed of carved basalt stones of various sizes and weights. Some are light enough that a single person would have been able to carry them, while others weigh as much as 50 tons. It is unknown how the builders of Nan Madol were able to not only construct durable structures without the aid of binding agents like mortar, but also were able to move these great stones and sink them into the lagoon.

KINGS AND PRIESTS

Nan Madol became the most important political and religious center in Pohnpei. While the population of Pohnpei numbered around 25,000, only about 1,000 people lived at Nan Madol. Archeologists believe that one of the reasons it was built was to isolate the nobility from the commoners. The largest homes were reserved for nobility and those with high social status, such as priests and religious leaders. The remainder were for commoners who served the nobility.

The religious leaders of Nan Madol were especially revered. The city was filled with altars, temples, oracles, and mortuaries, and some islands were occupied exclusively by priests. At first, the Saudeleur nobility continued to worship the agriculture god Nahnisohn Sahpw, just as the legendary Olisihpa and Olosohpa had, but the large concentration of religious leaders and symbols led to the development of many different cults. Over time, as new nobility came to power, the once benevolent and gracious Saudeleur aristocrats abandoned their old ideas of morality and embraced crueler ideals. Nan Madol was dependent upon the Pohnpei mainland for all of its food and water, as there is no fresh water or arable land in the lagoon. The increasingly cruel Saudeleur royalty would purposely starve the native population, and the oppression led to immense unrest.

THE END OF THE SAUDELEUR

By 1628, the unhappiness and discontent of the Pohnpei people paved the way for an invasion of the island, led by a warrior named Isokelekel. Pohnpeian legend calls Isokelekel a demigod, who was angry with the Saudeleur royalty and their abandonment of Nahnisohn Sahpw. But whether god or human, Isokelekel, with the help of the oppressed Pohnpei people, overthrew the Saudeleur and ran them out of Nan Madol. For a time, Isokelekel and his tribal chiefs lived at Nan Madol, but the effort of leaving the city for food and water, along with a population decline, led them to eventually abandon it altogether.

Today, Nan Madol is one of only two major archeological sites in Oceana. The other, Easter Island, attracts 50,000 visitors a year and is well-known even to those unfamiliar with the area. Yet Nan Madol usually hosts fewer than 1,000 guests, and many around the world have never even heard of this ancient wonder. Modern Pohnpeians like to say that magic was used to construct the city of Nan Madol, and with no evidence to the contrary, who's to say it wasn't? This "magical" place certainly deserves the interest and attention of the archeological world.

A KINGDOM CARVED INTO STONE

Fans of the classic film *Indiana Jones and the Last Crusade*
will no doubt remember the last scenes of the movie, in which
the titular character discovers the Holy Grail hidden in a boo-
by-trap-ridden shrine called the Temple of the Sun. In the film,
the temple was said to be located in the Canyon of the Crescent
Moon in the Republic of Hatay. Of course, well-traveled filmgo-
ers recognized the façade of the temple as the famous Al-Khazneh, or The Treasury, one of the best-known structures in the
historic Jordanian city of Petra. But even those who immediately
recognized the remarkable carved sandstone Treasury may not
have realized that the city of Petra was once known as Raqmu,
and it was the capital city of the Nabataean Kingdom.

The Nabataean peoples were Arabian nomads who traversed the
desert in search of food and water for their animal herds. They
continually traveled back and forth on what was known as the
Incense Route, a trading route that stretched from Qataban, in
what is now Yemen, to Gaza on the Mediterranean Sea. Aromatic resins including frankincense and myrrh were transported
along the 1,200-mile-long route, which the Nabataean tribes
became quite familiar with. Since they were so adept at finding
water and preserving these locations, these peoples were able to
become prolific traders, carrying goods across the desert more
quickly and efficiently than others.

MASTERS OF THE TRADE

By around the third century B.C., the Nabataeans had
control of many of the major cities along the trade route.

Towns such as Haluza, Avdat, and Shivta became welcome stopover locations for those who were traveling the Incense Route. But these cities were not only places to rest and recharge before heading back out on the road; they were also important centers of trade in their own right. Travelers could purchase horses and trade goods, as well as find a comfortable place to sleep. But even more than comfort, the Nabataeans recognized the value of providing safety for the visitors passing through towns on the trade route. They began constructing forts along the route, to keep merchants and travelers safe, but they also began charging taxes to fund their hospitality.

Thanks to this tactic, the Nabataeans were able to grow their kingdom and accrue much wealth. By 312 B.C., a thriving civilization had developed in the area that is now Petra. They constructed their capital city, which they knew as Raqmu, in the sandstone cliffs of today's southern Jordan. Archeologists were at first perplexed as to why the wealthy peoples would build their capital in such a location, as the area lacks a natural source of water and is surrounded by inhospitable terrain. But the Nabataeans were experts at finding water, unlike any potential enemies from outside the area, and the harsh environment gave them a natural defense against enemies.

FORGOTTEN, THEN FOUND

At its height, Petra was believed to be home to 20,000 inhabitants. For a while, the Nabataeans' strategy of living in such a hostile environment paid off, as even the Romans, who attempted to lay siege to the capital in 62 B.C., gave up when they ran out of supplies and could no longer handle the difficult terrain. But by A.D. 106, Rome had succeeded in annexing the Nabataean kingdom, and the Nabataean people gradually lost the control they had over the Incense Route. The Syrian city of Palmyra became the new center of trade in the region, and over time, the Nabataean people became scattered and powerless, until, by the seventh century, they were forgotten altogether.

In the 19th century, Swiss explorer Johann Ludwig Burckhardt rediscovered the city of Petra, and reignited interest in the lost Nabataean kingdom. In addition to Petra, many ancient Nabataean sites have been discovered by researchers, located along what used to be the Incense Route. The ruins of Haluza, Avdat, and Shivta lie in the Negev Desert of Israel, while other sites are located in Saudi Arabia, Syria, and Egypt.

But perhaps none of the sites are as well-preserved, or well-known, as Petra, which attracts more than a million visitors every year. To reach the city, visitors must traverse a three-quarters-mile long gorge called the Siq. At the end of the dark, high-walled, narrow gorge, the magnificent Al-Khazneh, thought to be a mausoleum for a Nabataean king, comes into view. The site is also known for Ad-Deir, or The Monastery, the largest structure in Petra at 148 feet tall and 160 feet wide. Thanks to the Nabataean peoples' skills in architecture and stonemasonry, marks of their once-great existence have literally been set in stone.

An Oasis in the Desert

The Oxus civilization was a Bronze Age culture dating back to between 2300 and 1700 B.C., and is sometimes also known by the more elaborate name "Bactria-Margiana Archeological Complex." "Bactria" was the Greek name for northern Afghanistan and northeast Iran, and "Margiana" referred to what is today Turkmenistan and Uzbekistan. And flowing through this Central Asian region is the Amu Darya River, historically known as the Oxus.

Although the site was first discovered in the 1970s by Soviet archeologist Viktor Sarianidi, the 1979 Iran revolution and the Soviet invasion of Afghanistan prevented many of his findings from catching the attention of Western researchers. But Sarianidi's discoveries would eventually amaze the archeological world.

Sarianidi had first discovered many Bronze-Age sites dating back to the 2nd and 3rd millennia B.C., as well as graves full of large amounts of gold, in the region of ancient Bactria. These sites contained structures with thick fortification walls, buttresses, and gates, and were filled with art of a very distinctive style. Shortly after, Sarianidi was conducting another excavation in the hot, dusty, Kara-Kum desert in eastern Turkmenistan. The flat plain of the desert contained a large expanse of mounds, indicating the presence of man-made structures that had long been buried by the elements. The site was so expansive, in fact, that Sarianidi assumed it had been occupied as recently as medieval times. But while digging in the region, he was surprised to discover pottery that resembled the artistic style of ancient Bactria.

NEW RESEARCH, OLD ARTIFACTS

The war in Afghanistan soon forced Sarianidi to abandon this site and explore other areas, but he made note of the sprawling, buried city, which the locals called Gonur. After the collapse of the Soviet Union, Western archeologists began to hear about Sarianidi's findings, and they not only traveled to the region to conduct their own research, but they also brought along more advanced technology than had been available to the Soviets. Sarianidi, meanwhile, began excavating the ruins buried beneath the desert, discovering a walled citadel nested within a larger wall, and a vast oval wall surrounding the entire complex. The Western researchers were able to date the city back to 2000 B.C., much earlier than Sarianidi had originally guessed.

The archeological teams also uncovered many pieces of intricate jewelry made of metal, including gold and silver, and semi-precious stones like lapis lazuli and carnelian. The sophisticated pieces, which often featured geometric designs, humanoid figures, animals, or mythical monsters, hinted at the skilled craftsmen who must have once occupied the area. The find also helped to solve an old archeological puzzle. For decades, researchers had found items displaying the same style as the artifacts found in Gonur in regions like Mesopotamia, the Persian Gulf, and the Mohenjo Daro site in Pakistan, but they were mystified by their origin. Finding a treasure trove of such items in Gonur seemed to confirm that their origin had been found.

OXUS ORIGINS

But Gonur was not the first settlement of the Oxus civilization. Researchers believe that its origins lie in the foothills of the Kopet-Dag mountain range near the city of Ashgabat in Turkmenistan. Here, in Anau, archeologists found more of the same ancient mounds found in Gonur, dating back to 2300 B.C., a mere three centuries after the Egyptian pyramids were finished. Researchers theorize that prior to Anau, small bands of people lived in the mountains of Kopet-Dag, where they established small towns and began creating rudimentary pottery that would eventually evolve into the more sophisticated pieces found at Gonur. This small civilization grew stronger, larger, and more structured, then expanded throughout Turkmenistan, eventually extending into Iran, Afghanistan, and Uzbekistan.

Although today the Kara-Kum desert can be a dry, dusty, and unforgivingly hot place, archeologists believe that when the Oxus civilization was expanding, the climate was more temperate, with more rain and more greenery. Oases along the Murgab River, which flows from the mountains of the Hindu Kush, would have provided the irrigation needed for the civilization to grow the wheat, barley, lentils, and fruits that they cultivated. In addition to engaging in agriculture, the civilization also created their impressive jewelry and pottery, and raised goats, sheep, oxen, and camels.

GOLDEN BOWLS

Along with the excavations of Gonur and Anau, researchers have made many more discoveries concerning the Oxus civilization, some deliberately, and some accidentally. The first evidence of the culture in northern Afghanistan was uncovered even before Sarianidi began his own investigations in the country. In 1966, farmers near the Afghan village of Fullol stumbled upon a grave that contained golden bowls depicting animal imagery as well as numerous silver cups and bowls. Not realizing what they'd found, the farmers began crudely removing the pieces with an ax. Luckily, local authorities got word of the amateur excavation and managed to salvage several of the priceless artifacts before they were damaged. They turned out to date back to 2200 B.C., and their distinctive style was eventually linked to the Oxus civilization.

The bowls were fascinating not just because they were crafted from precious metals thousands of years ago in the Oxus style, but also because some of the motifs they displayed suggested interaction with outside cultures. One of the designs was the image of a bearded bull, a theme that was common in Mesopotamia far to the west. Other patterns were common in what is now Pakistan, far to the southeast. This suggested that the Oxus civilization was engaged in trade with these cultures, to which it probably offered its own wares made of lapis lazuli, mined in the mountains of the Badakhshan province.

THE CAPITAL AND THE CANNABIS

But perhaps no place has served to reveal as much about the Oxus culture as Gonur itself, which many consider to be the "capital" of the civilization. Covering about 136 acres, Gonur is divided into three sections: Gonur North, Gonur South, and the Large Necropolis. Gonur North features the huge walled citadel that Sarianidi first uncovered in the late 1980s, which spans 330 feet by 590 feet. It also contains temples, water reservoirs, and a royal palace, which features two courtyards and an inner chamber that may have been a throne room or audience hall. Also found in Gonur North is a royal necropolis, where eight underground burial pits were found which contained numerous items of gold, silver, bronze, and ivory, reflecting the elite status of those who were buried there. Gonur South is a smaller complex surrounded by walls flanked with round towers. A shrine called the *Temenos* is located here, and within the shrine is a smaller fort in the shape of a cruciform.

The Large Necropolis covers about 24 acres and contains more than 3,000 graves of adults and older children. Young children were found to have been buried near houses or within buildings. The necropolis is notable for its mosaics, which decorate some of the walls as well as containers and boxes that were used to hold offerings of gold and silver.

Sarianidi made another interesting discovery in Gonur when he found what seemed to be a boiler for making *soma*, a type of ritualistic drink. He also found bowls with the residue of cannabis, opium, and ephedra, which may have been the ingredients for this drink, as well as mortars and pestles for extracting the plants' juices.

If soma did, indeed, contain these various substances, it would explain why the drink often resulted in hallucinations. But a definitive recipe for soma has never been found, and a positive identification of the residue Sarianidi found in the bowls has never been completed. However, most researchers agree that soma was made with some combination of plants with psychoactive properties, so it is plausible to imagine that the archeologist confirmed the use of these ingredients in the drink.

SHARING FAITH AND CULTURE

The Oxus civilization not only engaged in the ritualistic consumption of *soma*, but it also adhered to a religion that Sarianidi believed eventually evolved into Zoroastrianism, sometimes considered the world's first monotheistic religion. Oxus artifacts have been found in the Indus Valley, the Iranian Plateau, and the Persian Gulf, evidence of their interaction and trade with these peoples. It is possible that they also traded ideas about their faith, which, sometime before 500 B.C., morphed into what is today known as Zoroastrianism. Some historians even believe that Zoroaster himself may have lived in Margiana.

The influence of the Oxus civilization in Bactria and Margiana is undeniable. The peoples lived in meticulously designed cities with homes, temples, streets, and sophisticated irrigation and drainage systems. They were experts at cultivating fruits and grains in the oases of the desert. They traded gold, silver, and semi-precious stones with cities far and wide, while also sharing their ideas about religion. But around 1900 B.C., the cities of the Oxus civilization began to decrease in size, and within a few centuries, they simply vanished. As is the case with so many ancient civilizations, the cause of their disappearance is unknown. But they left behind many echoes of their culture, to remind us that even when civilizations disappear, they do not have to be forgotten.

THE SUBMERGED CITY OF PAVLOPETRI

In 1904, a Greek geologist named Fokion Negri thought he saw something that looked like the ruins of a city lurking in the blue waters of the Mediterranean Sea just off the coast of the Peloponnese peninsula in Greece. He noted the location of the curious underwater formations, somewhere between the island of Elafonisos and a small beach known as Punta, but it seemed that a simple report marked the end of his investigation.

Decades later, in 1967, British marine geo-archeologist Nicholas Flemming returned to this site and discovered a submerged city underneath 12 feet of water. With the help of Greek professor Angelos Delivorias and a team of archeologists from the University of Cambridge, Flemming mapped out the underwater city, now known as Pavlopetri. Buildings, streets, and public squares were all evident below the waves, in spite of the inevitable erosion that occurred after the city met its watery fate.

SIGNIFICANT DISCOVERIES

At first, the ruins were believed to be from the Mycenaean Period, the last phase of the Bronze Age in Greece that lasted from about 1750 to 1050 B.C. But further research showed that while many of the buildings and streets do date back to this time, the area itself was first inhabited much earlier, around 2800 B.C., making it one of the oldest submerged cities in the world. In fact, some researchers believe that Pavlopetri is the oldest submerged city ever discovered.

Forty years after Flemming's finding, interest in the sunken city returned, and researchers studied the site in more detail. Using digital mapping techniques originally developed for the military, scientists were able to recreate a three-dimensional model of the submerged city. Fifteen buildings, containing about twelve rooms each, have been discovered, as well as a sophisticated water management system, complete with canals and pipes. The digital mapping also allowed archeologists to see tombs and religious buildings, as well as a clear layout of the city, still apparent after thousands of years. One of the most impressive finds was a possible "megaron," which, in ancient Greek buildings, was a large, rectangular room with an open porch at one end, sometimes supported by several columns. These types of buildings were occupied by the elites in society, suggesting that Pavlopetri was an important city during its time.

Divers, who had the help of special robots from the Australian Center for Field Robotics, discovered a large number of loom weights throughout the site, indicating that Pavlopetri had a thriving textile industry. They also recovered many pottery jars originating from Crete, which indicates that Pavlopetri had a significant trading relationship with the island, or perhaps that the city itself was considered a major trading port.

FROZEN IN TIME

Sometime around 1000 B.C., Pavlopetri began to descend into the sea. Researchers are not certain why this occurred, but most believe it was probably due to a series of earthquakes, some of which may have been as strong as magnitude 8. Whatever the reason, the abandoned city sank into its watery grave, never to be inhabited again. This has given archeologists the unique opportunity to explore an ancient city frozen in time.

Because the ruins of Pavlopetri are so close to the surface of the water—some of the larger structures are less than two feet underwater—they face many threats to their continued existence. Pollution from passing commercial ships, dragging anchors, shifting sediment, and looters looking for souvenirs are all dangers that must be addressed in order to maintain Pavlopetri's ancient ruins. In 2016, the site was added to the World Monuments Watch list, which was created by the World Monuments Fund, an organization that strives to protect the world's most significant and vulnerable historic sites.

Flemming, who has revisited the site in recent years, envisions the city as an underwater museum and park, which would allow careful protection of the area while still welcoming visitors to explore the amazing ruins. He also believes that exploration has only just begun, and there is still much more Pavlopetri can reveal to the world. As research and excavation continues, archeologists are excited to see what else may be waiting just below the surface of the sea.

Vijayanagara: An Architectural Marvel

On the banks of the Tungabhadra River in the Karnataka region of India lie the ruins of Vijayanagara, at one time the capital city of the empire of the same name. Founded in 1336 by brothers Harihara I and Bukka Raya I, the region was already a site of pilgrimage for Hindu devotees of the god Shiva and the goddess Parvati, but it grew rapidly throughout the 14th and 15th centuries. At its height, it was believed to be one of the largest cities in the world, second only to Beijing, with a population that may have surpassed 500,000.

Within Vijayanagara is the UNESCO World Heritage site known as Hampi, which was built around an existing temple complex devoted to Parvati. In fact, the name Hampi is derived from Pampa, another name sometimes given to the goddess. Archeologists have uncovered pottery in the region dating back to the 2nd and 3rd centuries, so it is evident that humans were drawn to the location long before the creation of the Vijayanagara empire. Local folklore tells a tale of two hunters named Hakka and Bukka who saw a strange sight in the area before humans had settled there. The hunters were watching their dog chase a rabbit across the land, when suddenly, the rabbit turned and instead began chasing the dog. Hakka and Bukka took this as a sign that they had found a unique place within India, and moved their entire village to the new location.

WORLD-RENOWNED

Whether or not the story is true, Hampi certainly did become a unique place in India. The city attracted people from all over the world, who came to the crowded markets where merchants traded and sold their wares for spices, cotton, silver, and gold. Art and architecture were greatly prized, and magnificent temples, forts, palaces, shrines, water structures, and gateways were constructed. By the year 1500, Vijayanagara covered 250 square miles and was the richest city in India.

But as the saying goes, all good things must come to an end; and Vijayanagara was no exception. In the 16th century, the city was engaged in ongoing wars with Muslim sultanates. Five of these sultanates, who were normally rivals, formed an alliance, known as the Deccan sultanates, just north of Vijayanagara. Together, they attacked the city in January 1565 during the Battle of Talikota, capturing and beheading the leader of Vijayanagara, Aliya Rama Raya. The metropolitan city was looted and burned over the next several months, and was finally abandoned.

But today, more than 1,600 structures spread over 16 square miles have been restored in Hampi. These include the Virupaksha temple, known for its 160-foot-high *gopuram*, or monumental tower, and the amazing Garuda shrine, a large stone chariot often referenced as a symbol of Hampi. Also restored are public plazas, water features, kitchens, dining halls, and elephant stables. The once magnificent Vijayanagara, which attracted visitors from far and wide, continues to welcome people from around the world, who marvel at its history and architecture.

XANADU: CITY OF DREAMS

Fans of literature may recall Samuel Taylor Coleridge's poem "Kubla Khan," which begins with the lines:

In Xanadu did Kubla Khan
A stately pleasure-dome decree:
Where Alph, the sacred river, ran
Through caverns measureless to man
 Down to a sunless sea.

The poem goes on to speak of "gardens," "towers," and "greenery," describing the area as "enchanted." According to Coleridge himself, he wrote the poem one night after reading about Shangdu, the summer capital of the Yuan Dynasty which came to prominence under its leader, Kublai Khan. The poet also claimed to have partaken in opium, which fueled his imagination with vivid dreams.

Whether or not "Kubla Khan" was the result of a drug-addled dream, Shangdu, better known as Xanadu, was a real place. Shangdu came to be known for its gardens, waterways, and temples.

SUMMERING IN THE CITY

Located about 220 miles north of Beijing in what is now Shangdu Town in Inner Mongolia, the city was originally named Kaiping, meaning "open and flat," and was built between 1252 and 1256. In 1263, the capital of the Mongol Empire was moved from Karakorum to Kaiping, but just ten years later the capital was moved again, to Khanbaliq, or what is now Beijing. But Kublai Khan, who began his reign in 1260, enjoyed the cooler summer climate in Kaiping so much that he transferred his entire court to the city every year during the warmer months. He renamed it Shangdu, or Xanadu, meaning "upper capital," to reflect the importance of the city to the Mongol Empire.

Laid out in a square shape, the city was surrounded by earthen walls that were 12 to 18 feet high. Six towers were located on each side of the perimeter wall, just like the "towers" Coleridge spoke of in his poem. Xanadu was divided into an "Inner City," where the Khan and his court resided in a palace built of wood, stone, marble, and glazed tiles, and the "Outer City," where most of the general population lived in houses built of mud and wood. The Inner City was surrounded by walls made of brick which were 10 to 16 feet high, and four more towers adorned the walls. An abundance of natural springs provided water to the city, contributing to the "gardens" and "greenery" of the location. To the northwest of the city, the Mongols had created a preserve for one of their favorite pastimes, hunting, which was surrounded by another earthen wall as well as a moat. The preserve was filled with wild game such as deer, but also enclosed domesticated animals including falcons, horses, and cows.

A VISIT FROM MARCO POLO

Xanadu became known for hosting great feasts and hunting parties, and was a gathering place for the Mongol tribal chiefs, who debated how best to run their empire. It was also a destination for travelers who had heard the tales of great Asian rulers and their kingdoms.

Perhaps the most famous of these travelers was the Venetian explorer Marco Polo, who visited Xanadu and served in Kublai Khan's court between 1275 and 1292. He wrote of his experiences in Xanadu in his book, *The Travels of Marco Polo*. In it, the explorer described two palaces used by Kublai Khan: One a marble palace, complete with columns of gilt and lacquer, and the second built of cane or wicker and varnished to be watertight. The Cane Palace, as he described it, could be deconstructed and moved to a different location if the Khan so desired.

Xanadu embraced a combination of Mongol and Chinese traditions, which Kublai Khan believed symbolized the future. However, not everyone saw it the same way. Many Mongols thought the city was too Chinese, and they felt it was an abandonment of their own culture. The Chinese, on the other hand, believed the city encompassed a way of life that was too Mongol, and thought it should more formally adopt Chinese culture. Over time, bitterness, struggle, and discontent among the populace began to weaken the city. This, coupled with droughts, floods, and famines that plagued the region in the mid-1300s, led to the fall of the Yuan Dynasty in 1368. Although Xanadu initially survived the fall of the empire, it suffered a period of neglect and was finally abandoned in 1430.

LASTING LEGACY

The city was effectively forgotten for centuries, reclaimed by the grasslands of Inner Mongolia and mostly hidden from view. In 1872, an English physician and amateur Orientalist named Stephen Wootton Bushell became the first European to visit Xanadu since the time of Marco Polo. He described stone lions and dragons and a ruined palace strewn with marble tiles. By the time archeologists began to excavate the site in earnest more than a century later, much of what Bushell had described had been removed by inhabitants of a nearby town.

Even so, researchers have managed to uncover the ruins of more than 1,000 buildings, as well as the foundations of 700 other structures. Colorful roof tiles, marble columns, ceramics, jade sculptures, and coins have all been discovered in the area. In 2011, Xanadu, which is now recognized as a UNESCO World Heritage Site, was opened to visitors. The city has become synonymous with exotic splendor and mystery, and has been referenced in movies like *Citizen Kane* and, of course, the 1980 film *Xanadu*. Today, fans of Samuel Taylor Coleridge can visit the site of his poem's inspiration and imagine the grandeur that once enthralled travelers like Marco Polo.

EASTER ISLAND

On Easter Sunday in 1722, a Dutch ship landed on a small island 2,300 miles from the coast of South America. Polynesian explorers had preceded them by a thousand years or more, and the Europeans found the descendants of those early visitors still living on the island. They also found a strange collection of almost 900 enormous stone heads, or *moai*, standing with their backs to the sea, gazing across the island with eyes hewn out of coral. The image of those faces haunts visitors to this day.

ANCESTORS AT THE END OF THE LAND

Easter Island legend tells of the great Chief Hotu Matu'a, the Great Parent, striking out from Polynesia in a canoe, taking his family on a voyage across the trackless ocean in search of a new home. He made landfall on Te-Pito-te-Henua, the End of the Land, sometime between A.D. 400 and 700. Finding the island well-suited to habitation, his descendants spread out to cover much of the island, living off the natural bounty of the land and sea. With their survival assured, they built *ahu*—ceremonial sites featuring a large stone mound—and on them erected moai, which were representations of notable chieftains who led the island over the centuries. The moai weren't literal depictions of their ancestors, but rather embodied their spirit, or mana, and conferred blessings and protection on the islanders.

The construction of these moai was quite a project. A hereditary class of sculptors oversaw the main quarry, located near one of the volcanic mountains on the island. Groups of people would request a moai for their local ahu, and the sculptors would go to work, their efforts supported by gifts of food and other goods. Over time, they created 887 of the stone moai, averaging just over 13 feet tall and weighing around 14 tons, but ranging from one extreme of just under four feet tall to a behemoth that towered 71 feet. The moai were then transported across the island by a mechanism that still remains in doubt, but that may have involved rolling them on the trunks of palm trees felled for that purpose—a technique that was to have terrible repercussions for the islanders.

When Europeans first made landfall on Easter Island, they found an island full of standing moai. Fifty-two years later, James Cook reported that many of the statues had been toppled, and by the 1830s none were left standing. What's more, the statues hadn't just been knocked over; many of them had boulders placed at strategic locations, with the intention of decapitating the moai when they were pulled down. What happened?

A CULTURE ON THE BRINK

It turns out the original Dutch explorers had encountered a culture on the rebound. At the time of their arrival, they found two or three thousand living on the island, but some estimates put the population as high as fifteen thousand a century before. The story of the islanders' decline is one in which many authors find a cautionary tale: The people simply consumed natural resources to the point where their land could no longer support them. For a millennium, the islanders simply took what they needed: They fished, collected bird eggs, and chopped down trees to pursue their obsession with building moai. By the 1600s, life had changed: The last forests on the island disappeared, and the islanders' traditional foodstuffs disappeared from the archeological record.

Local tradition tells of a time of famine and even rumored cannibalism, and it is from this time that island history reveals the appearance of the spear. Tellingly, the Polynesian words for "wood" begin to take on a connotation of wealth, a meaning found nowhere else that shares the language. Perhaps worst of all, with their forests gone, the islanders had no material to make the canoes that would have allowed them to leave their island in search of resources. They were trapped, and they turned on one another.

The Europeans found a reduced society that had just emerged from this time of terror. The respite was short-lived, however. The arrival of the foreigners seems to have come at a critical moment in the history of Easter Island. Either coincidentally or spurred on by the strangers, a warrior class seized power across the island, and different groups vied for power. Villages were burned, their resources taken by the victors, and the defeated left to starve. The warfare also led to the toppling of an enemy's moai—whether to capture their mana or simply prevent it from being used against the opposing faction. In the end, none of the moai remained standing.

DOWNFALL AND REBOUND

The troubles of Easter Island weren't limited to self-inflicted chaos. The arrival of the white man also introduced smallpox and syphilis; the islanders, with little natural immunity to the exotic diseases, fared no better than native populations elsewhere. As if that weren't enough, other ships arrived, collecting slaves for work in South America. The internal fighting and external pressure combined to reduce the number of native islanders to little more than a hundred by 1877—the last survivors of a people who once enjoyed a tropical paradise.

Easter Island, or Rapa Nui, was annexed by Chile in 1888. As of 2009, there are 4,781 people living on the island. There are projects underway to raise the fallen moai. As of today, approximately 50 have been returned to their former glory.

EUROPE

THE FIERY CUCUTENI-TRYPILLIA CULTURE

What do communism and the ancient Eastern European civilization of Cucuteni-Trypillia have in common? Well, as it turns out, much less than the former Soviet Union would have liked. More than 6,500 years ago, before the earliest known cities arose in Mesopotamia, this civilization became one of the first examples of urbanization in the world. Primarily located in what is now Moldova, Romania, and Ukraine, the culture was discovered in the late 1800s by both Romanian scholar Teodor Burada and Czech-Ukrainian archeologist Vikentiy Khvoyka. As a result, the culture was named for the village of Cucuteni in Romania as well as the village of Trypillia in Ukraine.

During the Soviet era, the country took a great interest in the Cucuteni-Trypillia culture, funding excavations and research. At first, this civilization appeared to be a classless society with no private ownership. The Soviets called it "primitive communism" and praised the foresight of these ancient peoples, living in their long-ago utopia. But as excavation continued, the assumptions about the societal makeup of the Cucuteni-Trypillia peoples began to unravel. Archeologists were discovering huge buildings and technology that called into question whether this society was, indeed, classless. The discoveries were so unsettling to the Soviets that any scholar who challenged the idea of the civilization being "classless" was deemed an enemy of the state or accused of being a terrorist spy.

EARLY URBAN DWELLERS

Surprisingly, the fact that this ancient culture was able to cause such strife within the Soviet Union thousands of years after it existed isn't even its most interesting characteristic. Around 3,000 cultural sites have been discovered throughout Romania, Moldova, and Ukraine, stretching from the Danube River in the southwest to the Dnieper River in the northeast. During the height of its existence, around 4000 to 3500 B.C., the people of the Cucuteni-Trypillia civilization built settlements that consisted of thousands of structures. Researchers estimate that each settlement boasted between 20,000 and 46,000 inhabitants.

During the early era of its existence, the culture constructed mostly dug-out pit houses, then afterwards moved to above-ground clay houses with roofs of thatched straw or reeds. Later, they built homes by arranging vertical poles in the ground and attaching walls made of woven branches and clay. A clay oven was placed in the center of the house for heating and cooking. Using their building techniques, the Cucuteni-Trypillia peoples were able to erect large structures that could be up to 7,500 square feet in area.

FEMALE INFLUENCE

For sustenance and farm work, the civilization raised animals—including cattle, pigs, sheep, and, in later years, horses—and grew wheat, rye, and peas. They supplemented their diet with hunting, fishing, and gathering. Men and women of the Cucuteni-Trypillia culture had defined roles, with the men engaging in hunting, raising the livestock, and making tools out of flint, rock, clay, wood, and bone. The women made pottery, textiles, and clothing, and were also important leaders in the community. In fact, one of the most unique aspects of the culture is their apparent reverence for women. An abundance of statues and amulets depicting female forms have been discovered, with scholars theorizing that the civilization may have worshipped goddesses and been matriarchal in nature.

Cucuteni-Trypillia pottery and ceramic work is of particular interest to archeologists, who note the sophistication of the pieces. The Cucuteni-Trypillia peoples used temperature-controlled kilns to fire their pottery, some as big as 20 feet wide. Much of the pottery was intricately decorated with patterns, designs, or depictions of female figures, with minerals and other organic materials used to create different colors. The pottery was so well-made that even modern craftsmen have had a difficult time attempting to recreate it.

BURN IT DOWN

But perhaps the most unusual characteristic of the Cucuteni-Trypillia civilization was their perplexing habit of intentionally burning their villages to the ground every 60 to 80 years. Why, and even how, they did this is mostly unknown. Entire settlements were torched, requiring a huge amount of fuel and the cooperation of everyone in the community. Interestingly, the clay ovens located in the middle of each home were often removed from the house before the conflagration ensued. Some theorize that the oven symbolized the "heart" of the home, and by removing it, the home "died" before it burned. The culture may have even believed that inanimate objects, such as houses, had souls, and burning them was a sort of ritual sacrifice.

Other theories for burning the settlements include a desire for urban renewal, a belief that a "fresh start" was needed at regular intervals, or simply a need to get rid of bugs or disease. One of the most striking examples of this practice is located in Poduri, Romania, where archeologists uncovered thirteen distinctive layers of a single village, indicating it had been burned and rebuilt the same number of times.

The Cucuteni-Trypillia culture's interest in fire may help to explain another strange discovery—or rather, lack of discovery—about the civilization. Very few human remains or cemeteries have ever been found in the settlement sites, and the culture created no funerary objects for their dead. It's possible that this culture was one of the first to make use of cremation, or they may have simply believed that their dead should be "returned" to nature, allowing animals and birds to consume the bodies.

ONGOING MYSTERY

Sometime after 3000 B.C., the Cucuteni-Trypillia culture began to decline and fade away. Like so many other aspects of this civilization, researchers are unclear about the cause. Many believe another, more war-like civilization may have crossed paths with the peaceful Cucuteni-Trypillia, driving them out or destroying them entirely. Others think climate change may have played a role, as the culture was largely dependent on agriculture and a drastic change in growing conditions would have been catastrophic.

Whatever their reasons for some of their unique behavior, the Cucuteni-Trypillia peoples certainly made a name for themselves in the world of archeology. From angering communists to baffling scientists, this unique culture continues to fascinate today. With research work ongoing, archeologists are hopeful that the Cucuteni-Trypillia culture still has much to reveal.

THE GOLDEN TARTESSOS CIVILIZATION

The Colombian legend of El Dorado began with stories of Andean kings who were covered in gold dust as part of coronation rituals. But the legend quickly took on a life of its own, coming to symbolize mythical cities full of gold, which Spanish conquistadors and many treasure hunters took as fact. Over the centuries, many have searched far and wide for the gilded, magical El Dorado, but to no avail. This story, like so many others, has been relegated to mythical status; but it continues to fascinate modern treasure-seekers today.

Stories of treasure-filled cities are not limited to Columbia or the Americas. A similar civilization, full of gold, silver, and other riches, was said to be found along the coast of what is today southwestern Spain. This culture was called the Tartessos, and it spanned the southern edge of the Iberian Peninsula, where it first emerged in the 9th century B.C. Like El Dorado, the Tartessos civilization was almost a legendary, mythical place to the people of the Mediterranean, who often heard stories of the silver and gold that were said to be abundant in the area.

PHOENICIAN INFLUENCE

Tartessos was described by ancient historians and was even mentioned in the Bible. But 2500 years ago, this civilization vanished, giving it even more of an air of myth. It wasn't until 20th-century archeologists began to find evidence of this lost civilization that it became clear that Tartessos was, indeed, once a real place with a plentiful supply of various metals.

The Phoenicians are believed to be the first outsiders who discovered the indigenous Paleo-Hispanic people of the Tartessos civilization sometime around the 8th century B.C. They set up their own harbor, Gadir, corresponding to present-day Cadiz, in order to load up their ships with the metal goods obtained in the area and carry them back across the Mediterranean. The native peoples mined ore deposits in the mountain ranges of the Iberian Pyrite Belt, which contained copper, tin, lead, silver, and gold, and the Phoenician demand for the metals grew over time. Ancient historians recorded the great abundance of the metals extracted from the mines, describing silver anchors crafted to replace the stone and lead anchors of Phoenician ships, and claiming entire forests were cut down to fuel the constantly burning melting ovens.

Soon, the Phoenicians were settling colonies along the southern coast of Spain, with no resistance from the indigenous peoples. Paleo-Hispanic and Phoenician cultures melded together in Tartessos like the prized metals that were mined in the mountains. Populations increased rapidly, especially around Huelva and Cadiz, and word spread across the sea of a land filled with riches, fueling the legendary stories that would be told about Tartessos.

A GOLDEN DISCOVERY

Tartessos remained a legend for centuries, with little to prove it ever existed, until a remarkable find in September of 1958. Just west of the city of Seville, in a hill called El Carambolo, archeologists discovered a Phoenician funeral urn filled with 21 pieces of gold jewelry and artifacts. Weighing just over five pounds, the golden items included bracelets, necklaces, and rectangular plaques. While the style of the items appeared to be Phoenician, the gold used to create them was mined merely miles away. The discovery was the first to hint at a larger trove of treasures from the Tartessos civilization, and sparked an interest in more research.

Soon after, hundreds of grave goods were found in a necropolis near Huelva. Cremated remains were found with items like bronze brooches, jugs, belt buckles, and incense burners, as well as iron knives with ivory handles. Thousands of fragments of Tartessos pottery were uncovered throughout the region, some of which was handcrafted, while other pieces were created on pottery wheels. Many dwellings were found, but none large enough to be considered a workshop or manufacturing facility. This suggested to researchers that the people of the Tartessos civilization were self-sustaining and fashioned their wares in their homes, free from governmental or political control. But those who worked most closely with Phoenician traders were often the elites of Tartessos society.

The Tartessos civilization is also notable for its writing system, written in what is known as the Southwestern script. The writing is a mix of individual letters of an alphabet and symbols that represent syllables, known as a semi-syllabary. More than 95 inscriptions have been found, but so far, researchers have been unable to translate the script.

BURNED AND BURIED

For decades after these many discoveries, archeologists debated what had happened to the Tartessos civilization. Signs of a decline began around the 6th century B.C., when smaller villages appear to have been abandoned. The Phoenician homeland was eventually conquered by the Persians, prompting many Phoenicians to abandon Tartessos and return to the land of their ancestors, which may have been one of the driving factors in the collapse of the civilization.

But in 2017, archeologists made a discovery that shed a new and disturbing light on the last days of the Tartessos civilization. In the Extremadura region of Spain, just north of Seville, researchers uncovered the remains of more than 50 animals, including horses with hooves that had been deliberately and symmetrically crossed. The animals were found in a courtyard at the bottom of a large stone staircase. Also uncovered were bronze cauldrons and braziers, as well as intricately decorated bone and ceramic plates. To archeologists, the finds suggested a large, elaborate banquet, during which dozens of animals were sacrificed. At the end of the banquet, the entire area was set on fire, and then buried beneath 14 feet of dirt and clay, an undertaking that would have taken days of work.

The people of Tartessos seem to have been attempting to bargain with their gods, but for what reason? One theory is that earthquakes and tsunamis near the coast destroyed many settlements, which would explain why the remains of the sacrificial feast were found inland. Perhaps the Tartessos peoples were simply asking their gods to protect them in their new land. However, this does not explain why they then burned and buried their new home, or why evidence of their existence vanished afterwards. Archeologists believe that when ancient civilizations buried a site, it was to protect their relics from looters, and perhaps even to preserve them for future generations. The Tartessos peoples may have deliberately left us a time capsule. Undoubtedly, the legends and stories of this civilization are far from over.

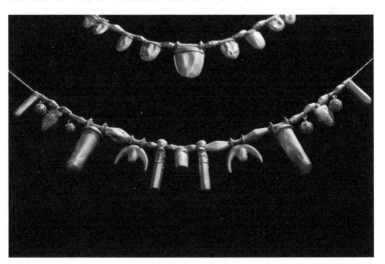

ROMAN PRECURSORS

Around 1000 B.C., the Villanovan culture arose in central Italy, becoming the first Iron Age civilization in the region. The name was taken from the site of a cemetery found near Villanova, now known as Castenaso, in northern Italy, where, between 1853 and 1855, archeologist Giovanni Gozzadini uncovered 193 tombs, most of which were filled with funerary urns. The area's natural resources were ideal for an ancient society, providing a perfect area for crop production. Without a constant worry about food, the Villanovan peoples were able to concentrate on other endeavors, such as manufacturing and trade, and grew their society quickly.

This civilization was the earliest phase of what would become known, by 750 B.C., as the Etruscan culture. Researchers have looked for clues that might separate the two civilizations, like evidence of warfare or migration, but have found nothing to suggest that they are not one and the same. The small villages of the Villanovans gradually grew, until they became the first major Etruscan cities.

INDEPENDENTLY WEALTHY

These cities were independent city-states, and they were scattered from the Tiber River in the south to the Po River valley in the north. Each Etruscan city developed its own industry, art, architecture, and government, so these achievements arrived at different times for every community. The cities located near the coastline tended to develop more quickly, as they had more interaction with travelers and outsiders, and they would gradually pass along their knowledge to the cities located inland.

The Etruscans engaged in trade not only with each other, but with tribes in northern Italy and the Alps, and with seafaring cultures that visited their shores, including the Phoenicians, Greeks, Carthaginians, and other Mediterranean societies. Etruscan land was rich in mineral resources, especially iron, which was offered for trade, along with wine, olive oil, grain, and pine nuts.

They also traded pottery, known as *bucchero*, which was considered their "national" pottery. Bucchero was prized for its black color, which was achieved through a process called "reduction." After a piece was formed from red clay, it was placed in a kiln and the vent was closed. This reduced the oxygen available for the fire, forcing it to draw oxygen directly from the iron oxide in the pottery itself. The finished pottery was a striking black color, which was then polished to a glossy sheen.

EASTERN INFLUENCE

By the end of the 8th century, Etruscan contact with outside cultures led to what is known as an "orientalizing period." Influences from the Eastern Mediterranean and Near East, including Syria, Assyria, and Egypt, first made their way into Greek art and pottery, and Etruscan interaction with the Greeks introduced them to the same ideas. Sculptures, ceramics, and metalwork all reflected this influence, but the orientalizing period also affected food, clothing, and religion.

Perhaps most importantly, the Greek alphabet, derived from the Phoenician alphabet, was invented during this time period. Thirteen thousand short Etruscan inscriptions have been found, most of which are epitaphs engraved on monuments. But several longer texts have been discovered, including the *Tabula Capuana*, a 390-word text that describes rituals to be performed at different times of the year.

THE RISE OF ROME

In the 5th century, B.C., Etruscan cities began to feature large fortification walls with towers and gates. The reason for this is clear to archeologists: Rome, at one time the Etruscans' smaller neighbor to the south, was beginning to grow larger and gain power. By the late 4th century, B.C., Rome had begun annexing Etruscan cities, despite fierce opposition from the Etruscans, who occasionally allied with Celtic tribes from the north in their efforts to thwart the Romans. For more than 200 years, battles raged between the ever-shrinking Etruscan cities and the growing empire of Rome. The independent organization of the Etruscan cities, once a unique aspect of their society, proved to hasten their downfall, as there was no centralized political unity amongst the peoples.

By 27 B.C., the last of the Etruscan cities had been annexed by Rome, which replaced the culture with Latin culture and language. The civilization of the Etruscans was all but forgotten for nearly 2,000 years. Luckily, the amazing artifacts uncovered by archeologists—including bronze statues, gold jewelry, intricately carved sarcophagi, and colorful tomb wall paintings—have given researchers insight into this once-powerful culture.

Today, the small town of Civita di Bagnoregio, located 75 miles north of Rome, is one of the best-known Etruscan cities that still contains evidence of its founders in many locations. From the layout of the village—which is in an Etruscan style—to the *Bucaione*—an ancient tunnel carved through the lowest part of the city—signs of the Etruscans are everywhere. While Rome may have silenced this civilization for millennia, modern history buffs now have plenty of opportunity to learn about the ancient Etruscan culture.

THE END OF AN ERA

It was called the "Bronze Age" for a reason: This historical period, which began around 3300 B.C., was characterized by its widespread use of bronze, a metal that was much stronger and more durable than other metals available at the time. But as the Bronze Age segued into the Iron Age, a strange shift occurred, leaving an inexplicable wake of collapse and destruction behind.

HUMAN INNOVATION

The oldest bronze artifacts discovered date back to 4500 B.C. and were found at an archeological site in Serbia. Before this point in time, artifacts were most commonly made of materials like stone and wood, and for good reason: Creating bronze requires a certain amount of knowledge and skill, unfamiliar to earlier humans. The metal consists of mostly copper, with between 5 and 15 percent of another metal—usually tin—mixed in. The tin must be mined and melted down separately, then added to the melted copper.

Over the millennium between 4500 and 3500 B.C., this technique became more common throughout the Mediterranean. By 3300 B.C., the region had also made advancements in culture, art, architecture, politics, warfare, and trade, and began to develop writing systems. Now-famous structures like the Pyramids of Giza and the Temple of Karnak were soon constructed, and civilizations covering Anatolia, Cyprus, Syria, and Greece flourished. The Bronze Age had begun. But sometime between the 13th and 12th centuries B.C., this age of prosperity and advancement suddenly—and, many believe, violently—fell apart. Within 50 years, cities were destroyed or abandoned, trade routes collapsed, and the newly acquired literacy in the area was severely diminished. What could cause such an abrupt turnaround in what had seemed an era of innovation and progress?

EVIDENCE OF CATASTROPHE

Throughout the Mediterranean, there is evidence that something catastrophic occurred at the end of the Bronze Age. In Anatolia, archeologists have found a destruction layer, or a layer within the rock or soil that shows evidence of disaster, in every major site uncovered. The Hittite capital of Hattusa was burned, abandoned, and never reoccupied. The city of Karaoglan, near what is today Ankara, was not only burned, but its dead were left behind, unburied. And the famed city of Troy was destroyed not once but twice, before finally being abandoned altogether.

Cities on the isle of Cyprus were sacked, burned, and abandoned, or were simply abandoned for unknown reasons. Archeologists found valuable items in many of these sites, some of them apparently hidden before residents left, suggesting they expected to return one day. But obviously no one ever returned to claim the valuables, leading to more questions: Why did the residents never come back? Were the citizens of these cities killed or enslaved?

Syria appeared to be a battleground for conflicts between many of the cultures in the region, including the so-called "Sea Peoples," an unidentified seafaring army that attacked many areas in the Mediterranean during the Late Bronze Age collapse. And in Greece, palaces were sacked and destroyed, with 90 percent of the settlements on the Peloponnese peninsula abandoned.

A PERFECT STORM?

When archeologists first tried to explain the sudden collapse of all these civilizations, they assumed the causes occurred in a linear sequence. Earthquakes, climate change, and famine could have led to social and political instability, which in turn led to mass migrations. The huge relocating populations then uprooted other settled areas, and eventually the disruptions caused a collapse within the entire region.

But not all researchers buy into this theory. After all, these civilizations had survived calamities, like earthquakes and invasions, before, so why would this time be different? Some scientists believe the more likely scenario is that the region was not dealt these blows in a linear sequence, but rather all at once. A city may be able to survive an earthquake and then later fight off foreign invaders, but what if they must handle an earthquake, a famine, and an invasion in a very short amount of time?

This theory is supported by Eric H. Cline, a professor of archeology and ancient history at George Washington University in Washington, D.C., who calls it a "perfect storm of calamities." If all of these disasters were to hit a particular area at once, they could cause a "domino effect," leading to the fall of other civilizations over time.

DROUGHT, INVADERS, AND REBIRTH

But the "perfect storm" hypothesis isn't the only theory suggested by experts. Some make the case for a widespread drought that forced relocation. There is evidence that tree growth in the Mediterranean had slowed at the end of the Bronze Age, and sea levels in the Dead Sea region were 50 meters below normal. A long-term drought certainly could've caused crop failures and instability in the region, leading to migrations and invasions.

Others attribute the collapse solely to the mysterious "Sea Peoples," even though this supposed group of naval warmongers has never been identified. But there is evidence that roaming tribes of seafarers may have brought destruction to parts of the Mediterranean, and, ironically, that they were bolstered by their use of new bronze weapons. But other evidence seems to suggest that the Sea Peoples were simply a migratory group of sailors who arrived at foreign shores with wives and children in tow.

Following the Late Bronze Age collapse, the region fell into what was known as the Dark Ages; however, all was not lost. Gold and silver craftsmanship joined bronze work, the Phoenician alphabet was developed, and eventually the peoples of the Mediterranean rebuilt their civilization. We may never know the true cause of the Bronze Age collapse, but out of the ashes of so much destruction came a renewed push toward advancement and the inspiration of unfailing human spirit.

RISEN FROM THE ASHES

On a regular morning in A.D. 79, residents of the ancient city of Pompeii, located near Naples, Italy, started their day as usual. The city had experienced several minor earthquakes that week, but nothing that seemed very alarming. In fact, earthquakes were quite common in the area, and the citizens of Pompeii were used to feeling a bit of shaking now and then.

They were also used to living in the shadow of Mount Vesuvius, which rises more than 4,000 feet above the Bay of Naples. The fertile soil in this area was used by Pompeii and its neighboring city, Herculaneum, to grow vineyards and orchards, and the two communities flourished, attracting merchants, manufacturers, farmers, and rich Romans seeking a vacation destination. They never realized that the rich soil around the mountain was the result of volcanic activity, as Vesuvius had been quiet for centuries.

So, no one suspected that anything was amiss that day, as they went about their errands and tasks. Bakers kneaded

dough and placed their loaves in ovens; café owners pre-
pared food to sell from counters that faced the busy streets;
children gathered in porticos to read Virgil's *Aeneid* as eagle-eyed teachers kept watch. No doubt many inhabitants
made their way to temples to give thanks to Jupiter, Apollo,
or Venus, while others headed to the public baths to relax
and wash up.

ERUPTION

But the quiet, normal morning soon gave way to a chaotic,
horrifying afternoon. Sometime between noon and 1:00 p.m.,
quiet Vesuvius suddenly became violent, exploding in a terrifying eruption that shot a mushroom cloud of volcanic ash
and pumice ten miles into the atmosphere, which then began
to rain down on Pompeii. Many of the city's estimated 20,000
residents fled in panic, but around 2,000 people remained in
the city, choosing to hunker down in stone structures and
huddle in cellars, hoping to wait out the eruption.

The next morning, an already horrible situation turned even
worse. Vesuvius first took out its wrath on Herculaneum,
which had been protected from the initial eruption thanks to
a favorable wind. But a giant cloud of hot ash and gas swept
through the town, burning or asphyxiating the remaining residents. This was followed by a flood of volcanic mud and rock,
which engulfed Herculaneum, covering it in 70 feet of debris.

Pompeii never stood a chance. Falling ash had already made
it more and more difficult for anyone remaining to breathe
properly, and buildings began to collapse under the weight of

volcanic debris. But it was the pyroclastic flows—rapidly moving clouds of superheated gases and volcanic matter that can reach speeds of more than 400 miles per hour—that signaled the end. The flows barreled through the city, with temperatures reaching 680 degrees Fahrenheit, destroying everything within their path. They resulted in instant death for those who had chosen to shelter in the city, and Pompeii was quickly buried in almost 20 feet of ash, pumice, and other volcanic matter. After two nightmarish days, Vesuvius once again fell silent, having completely swallowed the cities of Pompeii, Herculaneum, and surrounding towns.

RESORT TOWN

In less dramatic times, Pompeii was a resort city, originally settled by the ancient Greeks around 740 B.C. Over the next few centuries, Etruscans and Samnites enjoyed control of the city, but by the 2nd century B.C., the Romans set their sights on Pompeii, conquering it and establishing it as a Roman colony. The city prospered, and wealthy Romans flocked to the area for relaxation, indulging in its luxurious villas and elegant houses, which were filled with art, mosaics, and fountains. When they returned home, Romans would be sure to take a few bottles of Pompeii's delicious wine, made from grapes grown in the local rich soil.

The city was filled with artisan's shops, cafes, taverns, inns, brothels, and bathhouses. Communal areas included marketplaces, plazas, and a 20,000-seat amphitheater. While the elites enjoyed large houses, some as big as palaces of kings, the poor were less lucky. Many shopkeepers lived in tiny rooms above their workspaces, and slaves were housed in servant's quarters. However, unlike today, when those who are tightening their purse strings tend to avoid pricy cafes and bars, it was the poor of Pompeii who frequented the restaurant scene. With their cramped living spaces, the less fortunate felt that the city's cafes and taverns were perfect places to stretch out for a few hours.

BURIED AND FORGOTTEN

Vesuvius made no distinction between rich or poor, however. The extravagant houses and the modest shopkeeper's dwellings were all obliterated. And whoever was left in the city, whether man, woman, child, or animal, was frozen exactly where they'd been when the pyroclastic flow hit. Not long after the eruption, some survivors, as well as thieves looking for an opportunity to profit from the disaster, returned to Pompeii in an attempt to salvage what they could. Most of the city was buried, but larger buildings poked up through the ash, signaling where to dig for buried treasures. But once the salvaging and looting was done, the city of Pompeii began to fade from memory. After Vesuvius erupted again in following centuries, the city was completely covered, and even its name was forgotten.

It wasn't until the mid-1700s that the city of Pompeii was once again recognized. In 1738, workers were digging away earth to construct a foundation for a summer palace which was to be built for Charles of Bourbon, the King of Naples. They discovered ruins in the area, which turned out to be the remains of Herculaneum. Over the next several decades, excavations were conducted throughout the region, including at Pompeii, to recover artifacts. One of these artifacts was a stone tablet containing the words *rei publicae Pompeianorum,* meaning "the state of Pompeii." Finally, after almost 1700 years of obscurity, buried in darkness, Pompeii was poised to see the light.

GRAND VILLAS, COLORFUL ARTWORK

Excavations of the city progressed slowly, but surely. In the early 1800s, when the French occupied Naples, 700 workers were tasked with meticulously digging out the ruins. During this time, workers began to gain an appreciation for how expansive and grand the city of Pompeii once was. The ruins that were beginning to emerge from beneath their volcanic graves were impressive, and included the so-called House of the Faun, a large Hellenistic palace named for the bronze faun statue discovered in its atrium, and the House of the Surgeon, in which rooms full of ancient surgical instruments were found.

Over the centuries since excavations first started, more and more of Pompeii's secrets have been revealed. There is the House of the Tragic Poet, dating back to the 2nd century B.C., famous for featuring more than twenty colorful and elaborate mosaics and frescoes; The House of Julia Felix, one of the few Roman properties owned by a woman, who ran a bathhouse and rented apartments to wealthy patrons; and The Villa of the Mysteries, a large villa on the outskirts of the city in which well-preserved paintings on the wall seem to depict scenes of the Dionysian Mysteries, a cult dedicated to the god Bacchus. Homes, businesses, and public gathering places were slowly uncovered. The bakeries, butcher shops, laundromats, and hotels that still lined the avenues gave silent testament to what was once a boisterous, bustling community. Streets, including the main avenue connecting the east and west of Pompeii, the Decumanus Maximus, and the longest street in the city, the Via dell'Abbondanza, still displayed the worn-down indentations of horse-drawn carts.

THE VICTIMS TELL THEIR STORIES

While the ruins of Pompeii provided some fascinating insight into the lives of the people of city, one of the most interesting aspects of the area came from what was absent within the volcanic matter. Over the centuries, the ash and pumice that fell on the city calcified, forming a hard, protective shell around everything it surrounded. The bodies of the victims, entombed exactly where they died, eventually decayed, but the "shell" remained just as it had the day the volcano erupted. During excavations, workers would occasionally discover one of these voids in the ash, where bones would be found. In 1863, an Italian archeologist named Giuseppe Fiorelli had an idea. He realized that if he first injected plaster into these voids, he could recreate the forms of the victims, frozen in their final moments.

The plaster casts of the citizens of Pompeii have become one of the most fascinating and tragic symbols of the ancient city. Many victims were found lying face down, but some appear to be attempting to stand up or climb to higher ground. One person was found sitting, his hands shielding his face from hot ash or gases. Mothers were found next to their children, while couples were found in emotional final embraces. In one area known as the Garden of the Fugitives, thirteen people died together as they desperately tried to find a way out of the city. A slave was found still shackled to the wall of his master's house, a shameful reminder of the role slavery played in Roman times. Even animals did not escape the wrath of Vesuvius: pigs, horses, and a chained guard dog were all frozen in the volcano's ash.

The only known written account of what happened to Pompeii when Vesuvius erupted was recorded by Pliny the Younger, a lawyer and magistrate who resided in Misenum, located across the Bay of Naples. He wrote that he "could hear the shrieks of women, the wailing of infants, the shouting of men . . . Many besought the aid of the gods, but still more imagined there were no gods left, and that the universe was plunged into eternal darkness for evermore." While Pompeii and its victims were, in-deed, plunged into darkness for centuries, the work of hundreds of archeologists and researchers have once again revealed this grand city, and the tragic stories of its victims, to the world.

MYTH AND THE MINOANS

Greek mythology recounts the tale of the Minotaur, a fierce creature with the body of a man and the head and tail of a bull. To keep the beast contained, King Minos of Crete commi-sioned the architect Daedalus to build a convoluted labyrinth to imprison the Minotaur. The labyrinth was said to be so confusing and complicated that even Daedalus had difficulty escaping it after he designed and built it. Eventually, the Mino-taur was killed by the Athenian hero Theseus, who found his

way out of the labyrinth with the help of a thread he had tied
to a doorpost at the entrance.

While the story may be myth, King Minos and the Minotaur
inspired the name of the very real Minoan civilization, which
arose on the island of Crete and other islands in the Aegean Sea
as early as 3200 B.C. The name was popularized by Sir Arthur
Evans, a British archeologist who was one of the first scholars
to study Aegean civilizations. Evans is most well-known for
excavating the ruins of Knossos, a winding palace complex that
covers five acres and is composed of more than 1,000 rooms,
which has itself been described as maze-like and "labyrinthine."

EARLY, MIDDLE, AND LATE

Before the Minoan civilization began, the people of Crete
mostly lived in small fishing villages along the shore or farmed
in the fertile Messara Plain on the southern part of the island.
When the Bronze Age began on Crete around 3200 B.C., early
Minoans started to organize into centers of commerce and
skilled work. Evans called this era the Early Minoan period,
and much of what we know about it comes from the artifacts
researchers have uncovered from burial plots. The evidence
shows that great strides were made during this time in stone
working, metalworking, and pottery, and burnishing tools were
used to create decorations on these wares.

Around 2100 B.C. the Middle Minoan period began. Archeologists consider this the time during which the Minoans truly
developed a civilization. Populations increased, cities were

settled, and construction projects, like the massive Knossos palace, were undertaken. Crete and its resources were soon insufficient to support the burgeoning society, so the population began migrating to nearby islands. Some researchers further divide the Middle Minoan period into the "Old Palace Period" and the "New Palace Period." This is because of a large catastrophe that occurred around 1700 B.C., believed to be either an earthquake or a military invasion, that destroyed many of the grand palaces that had been built. These "old" palaces were then rebuilt into "new" palaces which were even larger and more magnificent than the originals.

Unfortunately, that was not the end of the disasters to befall the Minoans. The beginning of the Late Minoan period, about 1600 B.C., was marked by another catastrophe: the eruption of the Thera volcano, in what was one of the largest volcanic eruptions in human history. Once again, the palaces were rebuilt, but over the next several hundred years, earthquakes and subsequent eruptions of the Thera volcano—now known as the island of Santorini—caused a decline in the Minoan population until eventually the civilization disappeared around 1100 B.C.

THE PALACES OF THE TRADERS

But at their pinnacle, the Minoans had significant influence in the Mediterranean region. The civilization relied on trading for much of its wealth and economy, exporting timber, textiles, foods, saffron, and olive oil in exchange for copper, gold, silver, tin, semi-precious stones, and ivory. The Minoan trading network stretched from the Old Kingdom of Egypt in the south, to the island of Cyprus and the Levant in the east, to the Anatolian region of modern-day Turkey in the north. There is even evidence that their trading influence may have reached as far west as the Iberian Peninsula.

Excavations by Evans and other archeologists have given us a glimpse into the lives of these prosperous traders. In addition to the palace at Knossos, similar structures have been discovered at Phaistos, Zakros, Malia, and Gournia. Although they're referred to as "palaces," researchers don't know if the elites of society actually lived in these buildings, or if they were only used for administrative, political, and economic purposes. The palaces were often multi-story structures that were arranged around a paved center courtyard, and they featured indoor and outdoor staircases, lightwell openings, and sophisticated masonry. Huge storage areas found in some of the complexes suggest that they were, in part, used as distribution centers for agricultural commodities.

GROWING AND PROGRESSING

And the Minoans had plenty of agricultural goods to share amongst the population. The civilization grew wheat, barley, legumes, grapes, figs, and olives, and raised cattle, sheep, pigs, and goats. On Crete, vegetables like lettuce, celery, and carrots grew wild, providing more variety for the Minoan diet. They also domesticated bees and imported cats from Egypt to help control the rodent population. Their location in the Mediterranean Sea meant that seafood was plentiful, and fish and mollusks were regularly consumed. The diverse range of healthy food available helped the Minoan population thrive.

With the population growing, Minoan architects came up with clever systems for distributing water and for relocating sewage. Buildings were constructed with flat roofs and open courtyards that would collect rainwater and divert it to cisterns, and wells and aqueducts were located throughout cities to help manage water needs. The Minoans even created water treatment devices, such as pipes made of porous clay which would filter water until it was clean.

The thriving Minoan civilization also developed a system of writing, which may have been created as a way to keep track of inventory at the palaces. The writing consisted of both hieroglyphics, possibly inspired by the Minoan's interactions with Egypt, and a linear script known as Linear A, a precursor to the earliest known Greek writing. The language has proved difficult for scholars to translate, but much of what has been found seems to relate to accounting and recordkeeping. The scripts have mostly been found on sun-dried clay tablets, but writing is also found on ritual objects, pottery, and rings.

DEVOTED TO THE ARTS

Perhaps the most enduring aspect of the Minoan culture is the art they left behind. They were prolific artists, creating many paintings, frescos, sculptures, pottery, and jewelry. Some researchers are even convinced that Minoan artisans created art simply because they loved it, which would have been a major departure from the art that had been created before their time. Living in such a prosperous, flourishing civilization meant that citizens had plenty of free time to explore pursuits beyond basic needs, so many devoted their time to the arts.

Some art seems to have been influenced by Egyptian art, with human figures drawn in profile, but the colors used are often more bright and vivid. Bulls are found in many paintings, while the animal's head is used in pottery and sculpture, suggesting that bulls had some kind of religious significance. Marine animals are depicted in a large number of artistic pieces, so much so that "Marine Style" is a designation given to this art. Paintings of dolphins and pottery featuring squids and octopuses with swaying tentacles are hallmarks of this style. Ceramic and stone figures were common, including two figurines that Evans called a "Snake Goddess" and "Snake Priestess," but scholars are unsure of whether these sculptures represent deities.

Today, the largest collection of Minoan art can be found at the Heraklion Archeological Museum near the ruins of Knossos. Some scholars have called Knossos the oldest city in Europe, and there's no doubt that it was one of the most influential. While the story of King Minos and the Minotaur may be mythical, the civilization whose name they inspired has left real, and remarkable, impressions of its once prominent culture.

IRON AGE ITALIANS

Hundreds of years before the rise of the Roman Empire, the Etruscan civilization of ancient Italy began its own ascent. But before it reached its pinnacle in 750 B.C., the fledgling Iron Age civilization was known as the Villanovan culture. Emerging in northern Italy around 900 B.C., the Villanovans are considered the earliest Iron Age civilization in the country. The culture is named after an estate of the same name located near Bologna that was owned by Italian archeologist Giovanni Gozzadini. In 1853, Gozzadini discovered the remains of almost 200 tombs, which were mostly intact and still contained funerary urns. This was the first evidence uncovered of the Villanovan culture, which was soon found to have encompassed a wide swath of western central and northern Italy.

The two-hundred-year span of time before the Villanovans emerged is known as the Proto-Villanovan period. This era was marked by the development of agriculture and animal husbandry, as well as the discovery of copper and iron in central Italy. Settlements were established on hilltops and plateaus, which were chosen for their ease of defensibility, and the culture began to prosper.

BIG HOMES, SMALL HOMES

The Villanovans built rectangular, oval, and circular homes constructed of wattle and daub and sun-dried mud bricks. Wooden poles were added for support, and thatched roofs provided protection from the elements. Archeologists have discovered some remains of these houses, including the holes that were dug for the support poles and drainage channels that were carved into rock around buildings in which rainwater was collected in communal reservoirs. Some homes were also found to contain large earthenware jars sunk into the floors, in which food could be stored.

Interestingly, the Villanovans sometimes created small models of their homes which were used as urns to hold the ashes of their deceased. Since little remains of their actual houses, these models are often assumed to be replicas of what Villanovan homes looked like. The models feature decorative roofs and geometric designs on the exterior walls, perhaps mimicking the architecture used in real homes. Each model also displays a gap over the front door, which would have been a sort of "chimney" to clear smoke out of the home.

BURIALS, BELTS, AND BROOCHES

Archeological excavations have uncovered many Villanovan cemeteries, in which cremated remains were placed either in "house" urns or biconical urns. The distinctive biconical urns, which feature a small vase acting as a lid on a larger vase, were often decorated with simple geometric designs or human figures. Miniaturized everyday objects, such as knives and weapons for men and weaving items for women, were often buried along with the urns, suggesting a belief in an afterlife. Later burials eschewed cremation and urns in favor of tombs made of limestone slabs. In some settlements, tomb markers were carved out of stone and decorated with various patterns and figures, and some featured the depiction of a woman surrounded by animals, an indication that the Villanovans may have worshiped a female nature deity.

The Villanovans created pottery and metal goods with a high level of quality and sophistication for their time. Pottery was made by hand using unpurified clay containing mica or silica, and fired at a low temperature to create what is known as impasto pottery. Metal goods were mostly crafted with bronze, and included helmets, belts, buckles, shields, and sewing needles, but gold was also used to create hair pins, earrings, and brooches.

GOING THROUGH A PHASE

Some of the jewelry found at Villanovan settlements contains glass and amber, evidence of the culture's contact with other civilizations. Researchers describe this as an "Orientalizing" phase, where the Villanovan's art and culture began to pick up influence from contact with Greece, Phoenicia, and cultures of the Near East as they traded along what is known as the Amber Road. This trade route stretched from the North Sea and Baltic Sea, where amber was prevalent, down to the Mediterranean Sea.

With no evidence of migration or warfare within Villanovan settlements during the 8th century B.C., it is believed that the civilization simply matured into the Etruscan culture during their Orientalizing phase. In more isolated parts of the region, the Villanovan culture would last until the 6th century B.C., but eventually, it disappeared altogether. Soon, even the Etruscans would fade from memory, as the mighty Roman Empire began its domination of the Mediterranean.

SUNKEN CIVILIZATIONS

Researchers have discovered the tantalizing remains of what appear to be advanced Mesolithic and Neolithic civilizations hidden for millennia under water or sand. But are the ancient cities real, or is it just wishful thinking?

What is now the bottom of Italy's six-mile-wide Lake Bracciano was once a lovely and fertile river floodplain. In 1989, scientists discovered a lost city, which they renamed La Marmotta. Dive teams have recovered artifacts ranging from ancient timbers to uneaten pots of stew, all preserved under ten feet of mud.

The site dates back to about 5700 B.C. around the late Stone Age or Neolithic era. Though not much is known about the people who lived there, scientists do know that the city's residents migrated from the Near East or Greece in 35-foot-long, wooden dugout boats with their families. They had domesticated animals, pottery, religious statues, and even two species of dogs. They laid out their village with large wooden houses. Items such as obsidian knives and greenstone ax blades show that La Marmotta was a busy Mediterranean trade center. But after 400 years of occupation, it seems the village was hastily abandoned. Why they fled still puzzles researchers.

ATLANTIS BENEATH THE BLACK SEA

Ever since the Greek writer Plato described the lost island of Atlantis in the fourth century B.C., scholars have searched for its location. One oft-suggested candidate is a grouping of underwater settlements northwest of the Black Sea. Researchers claim this advanced Neolithic population center was once situated on shore along a freshwater lake that was engulfed by seawater by 5510 B.C. Ancient landforms in the area seem to have centered around an island that roughly fits the description of Atlantis. Similarities between the lore of Atlantis and this settlement include the use of a form of early writing, the existence of elephants (from eastern trade routes), obsidian used as money, and circular observatory structures.

ANCIENT ALPINE LAKE TOWNS

Today, most people would associate the Alps, the mountain region that borders Germany, Switzerland, and Italy, with skiing. But in the late Stone Age or Neolithic period, the region's lakes dominated the action. A dry spell in the mid-1800s lowered water levels and allowed evidence of ancient villages to surface within many lakes in the region. One site at the Swiss town of Obermeilen yielded exciting finds such as wooden posts, artifacts made from antlers, Neolithic clay objects, and wooden utensils. It is now believed that the posts supported large wooden platforms that sat over the water, serving as dock-like foundations for houses and other village structures.

HAMOUKAR: CITY OF COMMERCE

Until the mid-1970s, when the ancient settlement of Hamoukar was discovered in Syria, archeologists believed the world's oldest cities—dating back to 4000 B.C.—were in present-day Iraq. But the massive, 750-acre Hamoukar, surrounded by a

13-inch-thick wall and home to an estimated 25,000 people, was already a prosperous and advanced city by 4000 B.C.

Situated in the land between the Tigris and Euphrates rivers, Hamoukar was sophisticated enough to support commercial bakeries and large-scale beer breweries. People used clay seals as "brands" for mass-produced goods, including delicate pottery, jewelry, and stone goods. The city was also a processing area for obsidian and later, copper. The settlement was destroyed in a fierce battle around 3500 B.C., leaving more than 1,000 slingshot bullets in the city's ruins.

THE GREAT DANES

They sure ate a lot of shellfish—that much is known about the Mesolithic European culture that lived along the coast of what is now Denmark between 5600 and 4000 B.C. The now-underwater cities were investigated in the 1970s; the first is known as Tybrind Vig and its people are called the Ertebölle. The Ertebölle skeletons resemble those of modern Danes, but some also show Cro-Magnon facial features such as protruding jaws and prominent brow ridges. Archeologists have found implements made of antler, bone, and stone sticking out of the Danish sea floor. They also found large piles of shellfish at the oldest sites, indicating that the inhabitants loved seafood. Preserved remains of acorns, hazelnuts, and other plants showed their diet was well rounded.

The Ertebölle made clever use of local materials. They lived in wattle or brush huts; "knitted" clothing from plant fibers; made ceramic pots decorated with impressions of grains, cord, and bones; and created art from polished bone and amber. Eventually, it is assumed, the Ertebölle hunter-gatherers either evolved into or were replaced by people with farming skills.

MYSTERY OF THE BIMINI BLOCKS

The reason adventurers Robert Ferro and Michael Grumley traveled to the Bahamas was that they had read psychic Edgar Cayce's 1936 prediction that Atlantis would be found in the late 1960s off Bimini Island in the Bahamas. Needless to say, their discovery in the late '60s of giant rows of flat, rectangular blocks resembling a road off northern Bimini was a tad controversial.

The sunken, geometrically arranged rocks stretched for an estimated 700 to 1,000 feet. Several investigators estimated the "structure" dated back to 10,000 B.C. Since then, other explorers have claimed to find additional stones that may have once formed part of an encircling wall around the entire island. Author Charles Berlitz observed that the stones resembled work by pre-Incan Peruvians. However, geologists have noted that island shore rocks may split into regular planes due to a combination of solar exposure and shifting subsoil—formations resembling the Bimini Blocks also exist off the coast of Australia.

NORTH AMERICA

WHO WERE THE ANASAZI?

Across the deserts and mesas of the region known as the Four Corners, where Arizona, New Mexico, Colorado, and Utah meet, backcountry hikers and motoring tourists can easily spot reminders of an ancient people. From the towering stone structures at Chaco Culture National Historical Park to cliff dwellings at Mesa Verde National Park to the ubiquitous scatters of broken pottery and stone tools, these remains tell the story of a culture that spread out across the southwest United States during ancient times. The Anasazi are believed to have lived in the region from about A.D. 1 through A.D. 1300 (though the exact beginning of the culture is difficult to determine because there is no particular defining event). In their everyday lives, they created black-on-white pottery styles that distinguish subregions within the culture, traded with neighboring cultures (including those to the south in Central America), and built ceremonial structures called *kivas*, which were used for religious or communal purposes.

THE EXODUS EXPLAINED

Spanish conquistadors exploring the Southwest noted the abandoned cliff dwellings and ruined plazas, and archeologists today still try to understand what might have caused the Anasazi to move from their homes and villages throughout the region. Over time, researchers have posed a number of theories, including the idea that the Anasazi were driven from their villages by hostile nomads, such as those from the Apache or Ute tribes. Others believe that the Anasazi fought among themselves, causing a drastic reduction in their populations, and a few extraterrestrial-minded theorists have suggested that the Anasazi civilization was destroyed by aliens. Today, the prevalent hypothesis among scientists is that a long-term drought affected the area, destroying agricultural fields and forcing people to abandon their largest villages. Scientists and archeologists have worked together to reconstruct the region's climate data and compare it with material that has been excavated. Based on their findings, many agree that some combination of environmental and cultural factors caused the dispersal of the Anasazi from the large-scale ruins seen throughout the landscape today.

THEIR JOURNEY

Although many writers—of fiction and nonfiction alike—romanticize the Anasazi as a people who mysteriously disappeared from the region, they did not actually disappear. Those living in large ancient villages and cultural centers did indeed disperse, but the people themselves did not simply disappear. Today, descendants of the Anasazi can be found living throughout New Mexico and Arizona. The Hopi tribe in northern Arizona, as well as those living in approximately 20 pueblos in New Mexico, are the modern-day descendants of the Anasazi. The Pueblos in New Mexico whose modern inhabitants consider the Anasazi their ancestors include: Acoma, Cochiti, Isleta, Jemez, Laguna, Nambe, Picuris, Pojoaque, San Felipe, San Ildefonso, Ohkay Owingeh (formerly referred to as San Juan), Sandia, Santa Ana, Santa Clara, Santo Domingo, Taos, Tesuque, Zia, and Zuni.

AZTALAN: PREHISTORIC PUZZLE

Wisconsin's Aztalan was the fortified settlement of a mysterious society that worshipped the Sun. The Middle Mississippian culture erected stepped pyramids, may have practiced cannibalism, and enjoyed coast-to-coast trade. Some have linked the Mississippians to the Aztecs and even to the legendary city of Atlantis. All that is truly certain is that they lived at Aztalan for 150 years. Then they disappeared.

The site is near present-day Lake Mills and is now a state park and a National Historic Landmark. Still, what happened at Aztalan and the truth about the people who lived there are among the greatest archeological puzzles in the world.

Aztalan is ancient. During the period when it was settled, over a thousand years ago, gunpowder was invented in China. Macbeth ruled Scotland. The Orthodox and Roman Catholic churches split. Farther south, across the Mississippi from St. Louis in what is now Illinois, there was a strange, 2,000-acre city of earthen pyramids later dubbed "Cahokia." Its population was roughly 20,000—more than London at that time.

Aztalan appears to have been something of a northern outpost of the Cahokia culture. Because of location, archeologists call their civilization Middle Mississippian. They are distinct from the Woodland peoples, who were there first and remained afterward. The Mississippians were quite enamored with the sun, and at Cahokia, residents erected wooden solar observatories, similar to Britain's Stonehenge.

Like Cahokia, Aztalan was a truly weird place: 22 acres surrounded by a stockade with 32 watch towers, all made from heavy timbers and then covered with hard clay. Inside, pyramidal mounds stood as high as 16 feet. Outside the fortifications, crops were planted. According to Cahokia experts, the Mississippians were one of the major sources of corn dissemination in North America.

Today, Aztalan looks much different than it did at its peak. The mounds remain, and part of the stockade has been rebuilt. Also, the Friends of Aztalan group is trying to recreate antique agriculture with a small garden of gourds, squash, sunflowers, and an early type of corn, all planted just as the Mississippians would have.

GONE WITHOUT A TRACE

Another puzzle is why the Mississippians suddenly vanished from the Midwest sometime between A.D. 1200 and 1300. Author Frank Joseph has taken the folklore of three continents and made a fanciful case linking Atlantis, Aztalan, and the Aztecs in his books, *The Lost Pyramids of Rock Lake and Atlantis in Wisconsin*. Joseph postulated that the people of Atlantis founded Cahokia and Aztalan, mined copper, cast it into ingots, and shipped it back, fueling Europe's Bronze Age. After a cataclysm destroyed their Mediterranean island empire, leaderless survivors in the Wisconsin settlement migrated south. They created a new Aztalan in Mexico and became the Aztecs.

The Aztecs themselves referred to their far-away, long-ago homeland—wherever it was—as "Aztlan." However, scholars deny that residents of Aztalan ever used that name. It was merely a fanciful label applied by European settlers.

Joseph's evidence is circumstantial but makes for exciting reading. One of the great mysteries of Europe's Bronze Age is where all the necessary copper came from (bronze is made of copper and tin). Known low-grade deposits in Great Britain and Spain would have been quickly exhausted. Yet Lake Superior's shores have, and had, the only known workable virgin, native copper deposits in the world.

The Mississippians certainly knew that—they mined Michigan's Upper Peninsula. According to legend, Atlantis itself owed part of its great wealth to its trade throughout the known world of precious metals, especially copper. By bizarre coincidence, the Lake Superior mines closed precisely when Europe's Bronze Age ended. Another coincidence—it was at this time that Atlantis supposedly sank and disappeared forever.

There are many questions about the Mississippian culture, and answers are in short supply. According to the Cahokia Mounds Museum Society, archeologists have explored only a fraction of the site.

Aztalan became a National Historic Landmark in 1964 and was added to the National Register of Historic Places in 1966.

CHOLULA

In the United States, St. Augustine, Florida, is often cited as the oldest continuously inhabited city in the country. It was founded by Spanish explorers in 1565 and today it attracts visitors who come to see the historic sites, including some of the oldest houses and structures in the country. But this nearly five-century-old city seems positively juvenile in comparison to the oldest city in the Americas, the city of Cholula, Mexico.

Located in the state of Puebla, about 80 miles southeast of Mexico City, Cholula was founded as a small village sometime between 800 and 200 B.C. It slowly grew to an area of just less than a square mile, with a population of about five to ten thousand. Around 200 B.C., the civilization began constructing its most famous structure, the Great Pyramid of Cholula.

GREATER THAN GIZA

This giant pyramid, with a base stretching 984 feet by 1,033 feet and a height of 82 feet, was built in four stages and took hundreds of years to complete. At a volume of just over 5.8 million cubic yards, the pyramid is considered the largest pyramid in the world by volume, surpassing even the Great Pyramid of Giza at 3.2 million cubic yards. The pyramid was dedicated to Quetzalcoatl, an Aztec deity who was the god of wind, the dawn, arts, learning, and knowledge. In the Nahuatl language, the pyramid is known as *Tlachihualtepetl*, which translates to "made-by-hand mountain," an acknowledgment that the structure was built by humans and not the gods. By the Postclassic period beginning in A.D. 900, Cholula had grown to cover almost four square miles and had a population of approximately forty thousand. Around this time, the city was taken over by people of the Olmeca-Xicallanca group, who made Cholula their capital. But within several hundred years, the Tolteca-Chichimeca conquered the area and claimed the city as their own. Regardless of who occupied the city, Cholula remained a city of great importance to the people in the region.

THE CHOLULA MASSACRE

Sadly, in 1519, people in the neighboring state of Tlaxcala, wanting Cholula for themselves, convinced Spanish explorer Hernan Cortes that the city of Cholula was dangerous and conspiring against the Spanish. Cortes, along with Tlaxcala warriors, attacked the city, massacred much of the population, burned the city, and destroyed much of the Great Pyramid, reducing it to a hill of rubble. After the Spanish-Aztec War, which lasted from 1519 to 1521, the city was peacefully transferred to the Spanish, and Cortes built dozens of Christian churches to replace the pagan temples that once stood within the town. Although the city only contains around 50 churches, the number is unusually high for a city of Cholula's size. A popular legend claims that the city has 365 churches, "one for every day of the year."

In 1881, Swiss-born American archeologist Adolph Bandelier became the first researcher to study the ruins of the Great Pyramid of Cholula, and in 1931 excavations began in earnest. Much of the excavation required tunneling under and through the remains of the structure, allowing archeologists to map out the various layers of the building. Researchers were able to conclude that the base of the pyramid had been constructed from sun-dried adobe bricks made up of ceramic material, obsidian, and gravel. They also discovered numerous clay figurines, musical instruments, tools, and an ornate ceremonial scepter carved from bone.

THE CHURCH ON THE HILL

Later excavations unearthed plazas, patios, and courtyards that were part of the pyramid temple complex, some of which were restored or reconstructed. The pyramid itself, however, was unable to be reconstructed. Instead, the hill under which the pyramid now rests was topped with the Iglesia de Nuestra Señora de los Remedios, or Our Lady of Remedies Church, which was built between 1574 and 1575. Other discoveries made during the excavations of the pyramid include human remains, decorated altars, and painted murals. One of these, known as the Mural of the Drinkers, is the only mural found that depicts human figures. And, at a length of 187 feet, it is one of the longest pre-Columbian murals ever found in Mexico.

Today, almost half a million people travel to Cholula every year to see the ruins of the Great Pyramid and its surrounding structures. About five miles of tunnels have been dug by researchers who have studied the area, and around half a mile of them are accessible to tourists. There is also a museum that features a model of what the pyramid may have looked like thousands of years ago. Even as the oldest city in the Americas, Cholula continues to offer new experiences and discoveries to the curious visitors who explore its treasures.

A LOST CITY IN KANSAS

The State of Kansas, known for its agriculture and for being the home of Dorothy in *The Wizard of Oz*, is probably one of the last places that comes to mind when reflecting on lost civilizations. Yet Arkansas City, located in the southwestern part of the state along the confluence of the Arkansas River and Walnut River, was once the location of Etzanoa, home of the Wichita people.

The first record of Etzanoa can be traced back to 1595, when an expedition of Spanish colonists, including an indigenous Mexican by the name of Jusepe Gutierrez, happened upon a "very large settlement" stretching for miles along a river. Six years later, Gutierrez guided Juan de Onate, the founder and governor of New Mexico, back to the same area the Spanish colonists had explored years earlier. The men, along with more than 70 Spanish and Indian soldiers, priests, and servants, ran into a group of Escanjaque Indians along the way, who led the Spanish explorers to an encampment of another Indian tribe. Onate called these people "Rayados," using the Spanish word for "striped," in reference to their tattooed faces.

THE GREAT SETTLEMENT

The Rayados were friendly and helpful to Onate and his contingent, but the Escanjaque had an ulterior motive for bringing the Spanish to the settlement. The two tribes were enemies, and the Escanjaque requested help from the Spanish in attacking the Rayados. Although Onate refused to attack the peaceful Rayados, he did take their chief, Catarax, hostage and used him as a guide. Catarax led the group to another large settlement on the banks of the Arkansas River, where they found more than 1,200 round houses with thatched roofs, along with fields full of corn, beans, squash, and pumpkins. The people from the village had fled, however, fearing an attack either from the Spanish or from the Escanjaque.

Catarax was soon rescued by his people, and Onate and his group decided to return to New Mexico lest they face the wrath of the Rayados for taking their chief hostage. But on their way home, it was the Escanjaque who attacked, resulting in casualties on both sides. Onate was able to capture one of the attackers, and, still fascinated with the large village on the river Catarax had shown him, asked the captive to draw a map of the area. The Escanjaque complied, calling the village the "Great Settlement" of "Etzanoa."

NEW TRANSLATIONS OF OLD STORIES

Over the centuries, this story faded into obscurity, until it was mostly lost to time. The fabled "Great Settlement" was forgotten, even by archeologists, who had studied the area around the Arkansas and Walnut rivers many times since the 1930s and never found evidence of a single large community. Although construction crews, road workers, and even residents of Arkansas City had often found artifacts like flint arrowheads and pottery shards, they were assumed to be remnants of many different settlements and tribes. But Wichita State University archeologist Donald Blakeslee wasn't so sure. In 2015, he set out to prove that the huge settlement of Etzanoa was once located right in Arkansas City.

Blakeslee acquired newly updated, and more precise, translations of old Spanish documents and maps concerning the Rayados and Etzanoa. The documents, which had been compiled after Onate's 1601 expedition, described the geography of the area, the size and types of dwellings found, and the appearance of the native "Rayados," who, researchers now know, were the Wichita Indians.

The expedition members described seeing around 2,000 beehive-shaped, grass hut homes, spread out over a five-mile area on both sides of the Walnut River. The homes were approximately 70 to 80 feet in circumference, and about ten people lived in each home, making the population of the village around 20,000. Houses were arranged in clusters, and between each cluster of homes was land planted with crops. The women of the village tended to the gardens with tools made of stone, wood, bone, and deer antlers, and the men hunted for wild game with stone arrow points, knives, and spears.

A LOST SETTLEMENT FOUND

Blakeslee was able to decipher two maps—which were drawn in an unfamiliar and unusual style compared to modern maps, making them difficult for previous researchers to understand—and believed that they both pointed to Arkansas City as the location of the settlement. Over the next several years, Blakeslee, along with other archeologists and volunteers, unearthed an overwhelming number of stone tools, weapons, and cooking utensils that would have been used by the Wichita. But even more compelling, volunteers found horseshoe nails, bullets, and a cannonball, items left behind by the 1601

Spanish expedition during their battle with the Escanjaque. Blakeslee was certain now: This was the site of the legendary Great Settlement of Etzanoa.

Researchers believe that the Wichita inhabited Etzanoa from about 1500 to 1720, eventually moving south into Oklahoma but leaving behind traces of their presence. And the Great Settlement is still giving up secrets today, thanks to new technologies and innovations. A recent drone survey using LIDAR (light detection and ranging) methods concluded that Etzanoa may have covered even more ground than originally believed, stretching into Winfield, Kansas, about 14 miles to the north. And a study led by archeologists from Dartmouth College recently found several circular earthworks in the area, which may be the remains of Etzanoa ceremonial sites. While the modern world may now surround it, it seems the Great Settlement of Etzanoa still quietly stands, waiting to reveal more of its mysteries.

THE MISSISSIPPIAN METROPOLIS

The Mississippi River is the second-longest river in the United States, flowing from a glacial lake in northern Minnesota for 2,340 miles until it reaches the Gulf of Mexico in Louisiana. More than a thousand years ago, a Native American civilization arose from the areas around the river, eventually spreading out to the Ohio River and Tennessee River valleys and beyond. Known as the Mississippian culture, this civilization flourished between A.D. 600 and 1600. The Mississippian people grew maize, created shell-tempered pottery, established social hierarchies, and traded with other cultures from the Rocky Mountains to the Atlantic Ocean. But they are best known for constructing large, earthen mounds, on which structures like houses and temples were built.

The largest Mississippian city in which these mounds were built is located in what is today southwestern Illinois, across the Mississippi River from St. Louis, Missouri. Although the original name of the city is unknown, it was named after the Cahokia tribe that inhabited the area in the 17th century when the French first explored the region. Cahokia is believed to have been the largest pre-Columbian city in North America, at one time boasting a population of up to 40,000 people.

CITY OF GROWTH

Around A.D. 950, North America experienced a period of warming climate that helped to boost agricultural production of the maize, beans, and squash grown by the Mississippians at Cahokia. This also helped to increase the population of the city, as there was an abundance of food to support larger numbers of people. As the city grew, so did the earthen mounds—around 120 in total scattered over six square miles—that the Mississippians constructed. These mounds were carefully planned and engineered, and would have required decades of labor and a large workforce. Around 55 million cubic feet of earth was excavated and transported to the sites of the mounds using nothing more than simple tools and woven baskets.

The largest of these mounds is known as Monks Mound, a 14-acre platform mound with four terraces that was built using approximately 814,000 cubic yards of dirt, clay, and adobe. The mound is 100 feet high, 836 feet wide, and 951 feet long, giving it roughly the same base dimensions as the Great Pyramid of Giza. Excavations in the 1970s revealed what seemed to be the outline of a 98-foot-long temple at the top of the mound, believed to have been the largest building in the city and measuring a total of 5,000 square feet.

PLAZAS AND WOODHENGE

But Monks Mound was merely the beginning for the Mississippians' grand city. Monks Mound was in the central location of the city, and four plazas were constructed north, south, east, and west of the mound. The Grand Plaza to the south was the largest, covering 50 acres and measuring 1,600 feet by 900 feet. Built in an area that was previously covered in rolling hills, the land was deliberately flattened out to create a large gathering space for ceremonies, celebrations, and games. Other plazas were used for merchants, and the city enjoyed thriving trade with societies as far north as the Great Lakes and as far south as the Gulf of Mexico coast. The city had residential areas separated by common classes and the elite, an area set aside for growing crops, a copper workshop, and burial mounds.

One of the most interesting features of Cahokia, aside from the impressive earthen mounds, is the "Cahokia Woodhenge." These large circles of wooden posts were used as a solar calendar, where astrologer-priests would chart the heavens and track the seasons. During excavations in the 1960s, archeologists found the remains of some of the posts, made from red cedar, a type of wood considered sacred to some Native Americans. Five separate circles were found in Cahokia, one of which has been reconstructed, in a location half a mile west of Monks Mound, to simulate what it may have looked like a thousand years ago.

TOO BIG?

If researchers' estimates are correct and Cahokia grew to a population of 40,000, this city would have been larger than any city in the United States until Philadelphia's population surpassed it in the 1780s. This is an especially impressive feat considering Cahokia itself began to wane during the 13th century, and was completely abandoned by 1350. Theories as to why the city was abandoned include political, economic, or social problems, perhaps exacerbated by an invasion of outsiders. But some believe the city's huge popularity was also its downfall: more people required more resources, resulting in deforestation upstream from Cahokia. Too late, the Mississippians realized they needed to replant the forest that had once helped keep floodwaters at bay. Crops and homes were destroyed, and overpopulation led to unsanitary conditions. There is even evidence that human sacrifice became common at Cahokia, perhaps in a desperate attempt to appease the gods and save the city.

Whatever the reasons, Cahokia sat deserted for more than a hundred and fifty years, and then was repopulated by smaller civilizations until the early 1800s. Today, Cahokia is a UNESCO World Heritage Site and is frequently included on "must-see" lists for the State of Illinois. Tourists can visit a museum and interpretive center, as well as climb stairs up to the top of the famous mounds, where Mississippians once lived and worked. Thanks to the preservation of this site, visitors can imagine what life may have been like a thousand years ago in the largest city in the country.

THE COLOSSAL OLMECS

The Olmec civilization was the earliest known civilization in Mesoamerica, originating sometime between 1600 and 1200 B.C. The civilization may be best known for their monuments known as "colossal heads," which, as their name suggests, are giant human heads sculpted from basalt boulders. But the Olmecs weren't just good at sculpting; the peoples were also talented architects and engineers, had a rich religious mythology, and passed along traditions—such as the important tradition of drinking chocolate—to future civilizations.

In fact, the Olmecs are considered one of a handful of "pristine" civilizations. These are cultures that arose on their own, without influences from outside sources. Later cultures, including the Veracruz, Maya, and Aztecs, borrowed from many of the traditions of the Olmecs, including the so-called "Mesoamerican ball game," which became a popular pastime for later civilizations.

The environment around the southeast portion of the Mexican state of Veracruz, where the Olmec civilization is believed to have arisen, may have been uniquely situated to support a growing population. Well-watered alluvial soil and easy access to the Coatzacoalcos River provided the foundation for agriculture and trade, much like regions such as the Nile, Yellow River, and the Fertile Crescent of Mesopotamia, which saw the rise of other great civilizations. Today the area is today known as San Lorenzo Tenochtitlán, and it consists of three archeological sites: San Lorenzo, Tenochtitlán and Potrero Nuevo.

THE MOTHER CULTURE?

While today the contributions of the Olmec civilization on Mesoamerica are well documented, the culture was unknown to archeologists and researchers until the mid-19th century. In the 1850s, a farmer in Veracruz was clearing away forested land one day when he stumbled upon a strange stone sculpture half buried in the ground. The discovery caught the attention of an antiquarian traveler named Jose Melgar y Serrano, who excavated the sculpture and published a description of it. His description, of a "colossal head" now called Tres Zapotes

Monument A, was the first recorded evidence of the Olmec civilization, and the first hint to archeologists that something exciting was lurking in the region of Veracruz.

Gradually, more Olmec artifacts were uncovered, but archeologists debated where this newly discovered culture fit within the historical timeline. Some believed the civilization existed at the same time as the Maya, and some even assumed the artifacts were Mayan themselves. But in the 1930s and 1940s, two researchers, a Smithsonian Institution archeologist named Matthew Stirling and a Mexican art historian named Miguel Covarrubias, began to argue that the items being uncovered in Veracruz predated any other Mesoamerican civilization known. By 1942, the arguments made by Stirling and Covarrubias convinced Mexican archeologist Alfonso Caso to label the Olmecs as the *cultura madre*, mother culture, of Mesoamerica.

PRESERVED PROOF

While some archeologists accepted this declaration, others remained unconvinced for decades, even after radiocarbon dating provided more conclusive evidence. Then, in 1987, researchers made a remarkable discovery at an archeological site in the town of Hidalgotitlan. Known as El Manati, the site was once used by the Olmecs as a sacred sacrificial bog. The bog, with its anaerobic and temperature-stable environment, provided the perfect conditions to preserve the ritual offerings that were placed there by the Olmecs thousands of years ago.

Some of the objects discovered in the El Manati bog were dated back to at least 1700 B.C., bolstering the argument that the

Olmecs existed before any other Mesoamerican civilization. At the site, researchers discovered wooden sculptures, ceremonial axes, pottery, rubber balls, remains of infants, and even traces of cocoa drinks, all well-protected in the muck of bog. Of particular interest were the very well-preserved rubber balls, which were found to be made of a type of vulcanized latex. Vulcanization was a process that would be unknown to the rest of the world until the 19th century, yet the Olmecs had already perfected their own method. In fact, the name "Olmec" was an Aztec name that translated to "rubber people."

FROM FUN AND GAMES TO SOMBER RITUALS

These rubber balls are believed to have been used for what is known as the "Mesoamerican ball game," a sport that was played for recreation and also for ritual purposes. While the rules of the game are unknown, it is thought that it may have been similar to modern day racquetball, with players using their hips to strike the ball. The game was played on a stone ball court between teams of between two and four players. The rubber balls used were around 10 to 12 inches across and weighed between three and six pounds, and researchers theorize that players may have finished games with some rather impressive bruises! The Mesoamerican ball game became an important part of later Mesoamerican cultures, but some archeologists are convinced that the Olmec were the first to invent the pastime.

The infant bones found at El Manati were also an intriguing find for archeologists. Some have theorized that the Olmecs may have practiced human sacrifice, although the evidence supporting this is scarce. While it may be disturbing to uncover the bones of such young humans, there is no way for researchers to determine how they died. And unlike other civilizations that were known to practice human sacrifice, the Olmecs produced no art or artifacts that depicted the sacrifice of humans. However, archeologists believe they have found evidence that the civilization practiced bloodletting, a ritualized cutting or piercing of the body that was performed by many Mesoamerican cultures. Cutting instruments, including stingray tails, ceramic spikes, and cactus thorns have been found at Olmec archeological sites, leading researchers to conclude that these were used for the practice.

RELIGION AND TRADE

Regardless of whether the Olmecs incorporated human sacrifice into their rituals, the civilization left behind indications that they did practice religious ceremonies. The archeological site of La Venta has provided clues to these practices, as researchers believe it was used as a ceremonial center. The site consists of stone monuments, altars, plazas, and one of the earliest known pyramids in Mesoamerica, but is lacking residential structures. American archeologist Peter Joralemon, who studies pre-Columbian iconography and art, identified eight different supernatural beings that he believes were important to the Olmecs. These include nature gods like a water god and maize god, as well as beings known as the Olmec dragon and the feathered serpent. Some of these gods were later adopted by the Maya and Aztec cultures, as well.

Sometime between 1200 and 900 B.C., the Olmec had developed several major urban centers and began engaging in trade with other regions. This is evident from the presence of artifacts made of materials like jadeite and obsidian, which originated from the area around present-day Guatemala. Likewise, Olmec objects, such as pottery, figurines, and rubber, have been found at the archeological sites of other cultures.

COLOSSAL CREATIONS

While some of what researchers believe about the Olmec civilization is speculative and pieced together, most of what is known comes from the monuments and sculptures they created. Rock carvings, jade and stone masks, ceramic figurines, and carved wooden busts are just some of the works left behind by these skilled artisans. But there's no doubt that the Olmec's best-known creations are the aptly named "colossal heads" that they sculpted from large boulders. Seventeen of these heads have been found, ranging in height from around four feet to more than 11 feet tall, and weighing between six and 50 tons. Each of the heads depicts a unique individual, and each head is topped with a different headdress.

The significance of the colossal heads is unknown, but archeologists believe they may have represented powerful Olmec rulers, dressed in ceremonial headgear or helmets worn for war. Many of the heavy stone slabs were transported almost 100 miles, from the Sierra de Los Tuxtlas mountains, which would have required an enormous amount of effort for the ancient Olmecs. Such a difficult task would probably only be undertaken for a person of vast importance.

Exactly how the colossal heads were transported and created is another mystery to archeologists, but it would have required countless laborers, boatmen, sculptors, and other artisans, and a single head may have taken years to complete. The boulders were taken from an area in the mountains that had been affected by a volcanic mudslide, depositing the large basalt stones at the base of the mountain slope. The Olmec searched for stones that were already relatively spherical in shape, to mimic a human head. After transporting the rock to a workshop, the head was roughly shaped by chipping stone away, then rounded cobblestones were used to refine the shape further. Finally, abrasive material was used to create finer detail.

A LASTING IMPRESSION

Today, it is possible to see many of the colossal heads at various museums throughout Mexico. Occasionally, heads are loaned to museums outside the country for temporary display. But Miguel Aleman Velasco, the governor of Veracruz from 1998 to 2004, authorized the placement of many replica heads, which can be seen in locations including the Field Museum of Natural History in Chicago, Illinois, and the Smithsonian National Museum of Natural History in Washington, D.C.

Sometime around 400 B.C., the Olmec civilization began to fade. Theories for the decline include possible environmental changes that made farming, hunting, and gathering more difficult, or volcanic eruptions that forced settlements to relocate. But the end of the Olmecs was just the beginning for other cultures that were strongly influenced by their predecessors. The feathered serpent god, Olmec-style art, and the

Mesoamerican ball game, for example, were all adopted by later cultures. Some Olmec traditions, like the consumption of hot cocoa, have even survived into the present. The Olmec civilization is proof that the culture of ancient peoples is more than just ancient history; it continues to impact our world today.

THE LOST COLONY OF ROANOKE ISLAND

Twenty years before England established its first successful colony in the New World, an entire village of English colonists disappeared in what would later be known as North Carolina. Did these pioneers all perish? Did Native Americans capture them? Did they join a friendly tribe? Could they have left descendants who live among us today?

TIMING IS EVERYTHING

Talk about bad timing. As far as John White was concerned, England couldn't have picked a worse time to go to war. It was November 1587, and White had just arrived in England from the New World. He intended to gather relief supplies and immediately sail back to Roanoke Island, where he had left more than 100 colonists who were running short of food. Unfortunately, the English were gearing up to fight Spain. Every seaworthy ship, including White's, was pressed into naval service. Not a one could be spared for his return voyage to America.

NOBODY HOME

When John White finally returned to North America three years later, he was dismayed to discover that the colonists he had left behind were nowhere to be found. Instead, he stumbled upon a mystery—one that has never been solved.

The village that White and company had founded in 1587 on Roanoke Island lay completely deserted. Houses had been dismantled (as if someone planned to move them), but the pieces lay in the long grass along with iron tools and farming equipment. A stout stockade made of logs stood empty.

White found no sign of his daughter Eleanor, her husband Ananias, or their daughter Virginia Dare—the first English child born in America. None of the 87 men, 17 women, and 11 children remained. No bodies or obvious gravesites offered clues to their fate. The only clues—if they were clues—that White could find were the letters CRO carved into a tree trunk and the word CROATOAN carved into a log of the abandoned fort.

NO FORWARDING ADDRESS

All White could do was hope that the colonists had been taken in by friendly natives.

Croatoan—also spelled "Croatan"—was the name of a barrier island to the south and also the name of a tribe that lived on that island. Unlike other area tribes, the Croatoans had been friendly to English newcomers, and one of them, Manteo, had traveled to England with earlier explorers and returned to act as interpreter for the Roanoke colony. Had the colonists, with Manteo's help, moved to Croatoan? Were they safe among friends?

White tried to find out, but his timing was rotten once again. He had arrived on the Carolina coast as a hurricane bore down on the region. The storm hit before he could mount a search. His ship was blown past Croatoan Island and out to sea. Although the ship and crew survived the storm and made it back to England, White was stuck again. He tried repeatedly but failed to raise money for another search party.

No one has ever learned the fate of the Roanoke Island colonists, but there is no shortage of theories as to what happened to them. A small sailing vessel and other boats that White had left with them were gone when he returned. It's possible that the colonists used the vessels to travel to another island or to the mainland. White had talked with others before he left about possibly moving the settlement to a more secure location inland. It's even possible that the colonists tired of waiting for White's return and tried to sail back to England. If so, they would have perished at sea. Yet there are at least a few shreds of hearsay evidence that the colonists survived in America.

RUMORS OF SURVIVORS

In 1607, Captain John Smith and company established the first successful English settlement in North America at Jamestown, Virginia. The colony's secretary, William Strachey, wrote four years later about hearing a report of four English men, two boys, and one young woman who had been sighted south of

Jamestown at a settlement of the Eno tribe, where they were being used as slaves. If the report was true, who else could these English have been but Roanoke survivors?

For more than a century after the colonists' disappearance, stories emerged of gray-eyed Native Americans and English-speaking villages in North Carolina and Virginia. In 1709, an English surveyor said members of the Hatteras tribe living on North Carolina's Outer Banks—some of them with light-colored eyes—claimed to be descendants of white people. It's possible that the Hatteras were the same people that the 1587 colonists called Croatoan.

In the intervening centuries, many of the individual tribes of the region have disappeared. Some died out. Others were absorbed into larger groups such as the Tuscarora. One surviving group, the Lumbee, has also been called Croatoan. The Lumbee, who still live in North Carolina, often have Caucasian features. Could they be descendants of Roanoke colonists? Many among the Lumbee dismiss the notion as fanciful, but the tribe has long been thought to be of mixed heritage and has been speaking English so long that none among them know what language preceded it.

CULTURE OF THE CHEROKEE

When 16th-century European explorers first began exploring what would later be called the United States, they found a land already inhabited by a variety of groups. Among these were a people living in the southeast corner of the continent who referred to themselves as the Aniyunwiya, or "the principal people." Their Creek Indian neighbors, however, called them the Tsalagi, a word that eventually morphed into Cherokee, the name generally used today.

The origin of the Cherokee is uncertain at best. Tribal legend speaks of an ancient time of migration, which some historians have projected as far back as the time of a land bridge linking North America to Asia. Linguists report that the Cherokee language is linked to the Iroquois, who lived far to the north; others point out that traditional Cherokee crafts bear a resemblance to those of the people of the Amazon basin in South America. Regardless of their origin, the Cherokee held sway over a great deal of land when Spaniard Hernando de Soto made contact with the tribe in the 1540s.

De Soto did not find the gold he was looking for in Cherokee territory. What he did find was a people who had heard of his treatment of other tribes and did everything they could to hasten his exit from their land. They quickly traded him some food and other supplies—including two buffalo skins, the first European contact with the animal, which at the time ranged as far east as the Atlantic coast—and suggested that he might be better off looking to the west. With that, de Soto headed off. The total number de Soto found living in their traditional lands is a matter of speculation; the oldest reliable count dates from 130 years later, long after the smallpox the Spaniard left behind had wreaked havoc on the tribe. The disease left somewhere between 25,000 to 50,000 people alive after killing an estimated 75 percent of the natives.

CULTURE SHOCK

The Cherokee were quick to realize that white intruders were there to stay, and they did what they could to adapt to the changing world. On the arrival of the British, they became active trading partners, seeking to improve their situation through the acquisition of European goods and guns. They also became military allies—by many accounts, a trade at which they excelled—fighting with the British against the French and later against the colonists during the American Revolution. The British, however, always viewed their Cherokee allies with suspicion, the effects of which ranged from the occasional massacre to the imposition of treaties demanding that the British be allowed to construct forts in Cherokee territory. This ceding of property was only the beginning of one of the biggest land-grabs in history, culminating in the 1838 Trail of Tears, in which 17,000 Cherokee were forcibly sent west, resulting in thousands of deaths along the way.

Part of the difficulty with the early treaties was that the Europeans were in the habit of making them with anyone who claimed they represented the tribe; in reality, nobody could speak for all of the Cherokee. Their system was one of local autonomous government, with each village being responsible for its own affairs. The individual villages even had two chiefs: a White Chief in charge of domestic decisions and a Red Chief in charge of war and general relations with outsiders. The society itself was matrilineal and focused on a spiritual balance that the Cherokee believed existed between lower and higher worlds, with the earth caught in the middle. Europeans were ill-suited to understanding such a culture. In turn, the Cherokee realized that their society was ill-suited to dealing with Europeans.

CHANGING TIMES

Cherokee society proved up to the challenge, however. Part of the advance was because of Sequoyah. Sequoyah was a silversmith who devised the first syllabary for the Cherokee language in 1821. Although he was illiterate, he had observed the white man's system of written communication. His Talking Leaves system, consisting of more than 80 symbols that each represented a syllable of Cherokee speech, was rapidly adopted and soon the Cherokee had a higher literacy rate than most of their white neighbors. One immediate result was the publication of a newspaper, *The Cherokee Phoenix*, in 1828; it was soon renamed *The Cherokee Phoenix and Indian Advocate* to indicate that its pages addressed issues faced by Native Americans of all tribes.

Along with the alphabet, the 1820s proved a time of change for Cherokee society as a whole. Realizing that they must deal with the white man on his terms, the Cherokee had unified their autonomous tribes by the close of the decade, adopting a constitution that provided for a formal judiciary and elected legislature, electing John Ross as principal chief, and declaring themselves to be an independent nation. They took the nearly unheard-of step of sending Indian representatives to Washington, D.C., to persuade both the Congress and the Supreme Court that the United States ought to be held to both the spirit as well as the letter of various treaties that were signed over the years. However, despite favorably impressing many with the quality of their arguments, their efforts proved fruitless, and the Cherokee joined their Native American brothers—being treated as second-class citizens for decades to come.

The repercussions from the almost unimaginable changes imposed on the Cherokee as European settlers came to dominate the continent echo to the current day. However, Cherokee society has proved itself equal to the task, and today its people are the most numerous of any Native American population, and the leadership of various parts of the tribe continues to actively work to remedy past inequities.

IDOLS OF THE AZTECS

Flourishing between the 10th and 12th centuries A.D., the Toltec civilization was often lauded and praised by the later Aztec culture, who considered the capital city of Tollan an awe-inspiring achievement of human society. Of course, some researchers believe that the stories told by the Aztecs of the impressive and lavish Toltec culture were exaggerated, and the yarns they wove, speaking of extravagant Tollan palaces filled with gold, jade, and turquoise, were more myth than truth. But regardless, the Toltec civilization made an obvious impression on the Aztecs, who considered their predecessors master artisans.

In fact, in Nahuatl, the language of the Aztecs, one meaning for the name Toltec is "master artisan." Another meaning, however, is "inhabitant of Tula, Hidalgo," the region that was ruled by the Toltec at the height of their prominence. The civilization is believed to have originated with the Tolteca-Chichimeca peoples, who, in the 9th century, migrated from the northwestern Mexican deserts to Culhuacan, which today includes the area around Mexico City. This was where the first Toltec settlement was established, before the capital was moved to Tollan.

AS THICK AS REEDS

According to the Aztecs, the first ruler of the Toltecs was Ce Tecpatl Mixcoatl, followed by his son, Ce Acatl Topiltzin. But as with other accounts given by the Aztecs, these figures have been greatly mythologized, even at times conflated with deities such as the serpent god Quetzalcoatl. But archeologists have uncovered more than stories and myth, giving them more quantifiable evidence of the civilization.

Tollan, and its alternate name, Tula, can both be translated as "place of reeds," which was used to describe a thriving city where "people are thick as reeds." True to its name, the city grew to span around eight and a half square miles, and supported a population between 40,000 and 60,000 people. While the Aztecs spoke of richly appointed palaces, intricate jewelry, and cotton textiles in red, blue, yellow, and green, very few artifacts have survived through the centuries. What has survived, however, are two large pyramids, the remains of a large palace, a colonnaded walkway, ballcourts, and many residential structures. Also discovered are the ruins of a large workshop where the Toltecs shaped obsidian, mined from the nearby region of Pachuca, into arrowheads and cutting tools.

ART, OFFERINGS, AND ADMIRERS

Many carvings and friezes created by the Toltec "master arti-sans" are still intact today. The tops of the pyramids feature large columns, carved to look like warriors dressed for battle, which at one time held up roof-like structures. Interestingly, these columns are nearly identical, suggesting that the Toltecs had some type of workshop capable of mass producing these giant carvings. A 130-foot-long L-shaped wall, known as a *coatepantli* or "wall of serpents," stands near the pyramids. Similar walls are found at other Mesoamerican archeological sites, but the coatepantli is a Toltec invention. The walls depict animals such as jaguars, coyotes, wolves, and eagles, some of which are devouring human hearts. There are also scenes of skeletons entwined with rattlesnakes, which are believed to be depictions of sacrifice.

Toltec artisans were also the first in Mesoamerica to create *chacmools*, sculptures of reclining figures holding bowls or vessels, which were used for offerings to the gods. Offerings could include food, alcoholic drinks, tobacco, incense, or feathers, but later civilizations, such as the Aztecs, used chacmools to offer the gods human hearts.

Researchers are unsure of why, in the 12th century, the Toltec civilization began to decline, but they have found evidence of possible violence or war. Some of Tollan's architecture was purposely destroyed, burnt, and buried, and the Aztecs gradually looted the city. This was not done with malice, however, as the Aztecs held the Toltecs in the highest regard. Many of the gods who were depicted in Tollan architecture were later adopted by the Aztecs, including Centeotl, the god of maize, Xochiquetzal, the goddess of beauty and love, and Quetzalcoatl, the god of life and wisdom. And whether true or not, the Aztecs claimed to be directly descended from the Toltecs. They even coined the expression *Toltecayotl*, which meant "to have a Toltec heart," when referring to members of their civilization who showed courage or excellence. Whether the stories told by the Aztecs are true or not, the Toltecs most definitely left an indelible mark on Mesoamerica.

MOVE OVER, COLUMBUS

Most of us remember learning about Christopher Columbus and his famous transatlantic voyages. The explorer's accomplishments are certainly noteworthy: between 1492 and 1504, he traversed the vast Atlantic Ocean in what would today be considered quite small (and no doubt uncomfortable) ships, and visited many islands in the Caribbean, as well as parts of Central America and South America. While modern commentators often criticize Columbus and his actions, there is no doubt that his expeditions ushered in a period of European exploration that eventually helped create the Western World we know today.

Surprisingly, however, Columbus was not the first European to "discover" the Americas. That distinction could possibly be credited to Leif Erikson, a Norse explorer who reached the continent of North America hundreds of years before Columbus ever set sail. Exploration was in Erikson's blood: he was the son of Erik the Red, believed to have founded the first settlement in Greenland, and was a distant relative of Naddodd, a 9th century Viking who discovered the island country of Iceland. But according to oral traditions that were passed down through centuries, and written sagas that were later recorded of the events, Erikson also made a discovery of a previously unknown land. He called this land "Vinland," and researchers now believe that it was a coastal region of North America.

LAND OF GRAPES AND TIMBER

Two Icelandic stories, known *as Grænlendinga saga*, or the
Saga of the Greenlanders and *Eiríks saga rauða*, or *Erik the
Red's Saga*, make note of Erikson's travels, although the two
tales differ in their details. In the Saga of the Greenlanders, a
Norse explorer named Bjarni Herjólfsson was blown off course
while sailing towards Greenland and spotted an unfamiliar land
covered with hills and forests. He decided not to go ashore,
however, so when Leif Erikson retraced Herjólfsson's steps
years later, he became the first European to step ashore the
land. Erikson and his crew explored an icy, rocky area he called
Helluland ("land of flat rocks"), a wooded area he called *Mark-
land* ("land of forests"), and a warmer, lush area that Erikson
chose for his base, which he called *Leifsbúðir* ("Leif's camp").
The group later found forested areas of fine timber and vines
full of grapes, inspiring the name they bestowed upon the
place, Vinland ("land of wine").

But in Erik the Red's Saga, Erikson himself is the one who is
blown off course during a voyage, becoming the first European
to see and set foot on an unfamiliar land. In this tale, Erikson
and his crew discovered an inlet in an area of strong currents,
which they dubbed *Straumfjorðr* ("fjord of currents"), and
made their base there. In a warmer area further south, the
group established a summer camp where they discovered timber and the wild grapes that inspired Vinland's name.

In both tales, subsequent expeditions to the new land are
launched from Greenland. Norse colonists began to establish
settlements, met groups of indigenous people, and engaged

in peaceful trade for a short period of time before falling into conflict and violence. Outnumbered by the large number of indigenous peoples in the area, the colonists returned to Greenland, with ships full of timber and grapes, and abandoned their quest to create a new home in the "land of wine."

UNKNOWN LOCATION

For hundreds of years these stories were little more than anecdotal, but most researchers agreed that they were quite plausible. Piloting a ship through the open waters between Scandinavian Viking territories and Greenland would have been no small feat in the eras before precise navigation. Vikings relied on knowledge of tides, wind direction, landmarks, and even the movement of whales to help steer their ships, so it isn't hard to imagine that a bout of bad weather or fog could significantly alter a course. But finding actual evidence of these Viking voyages has proved to be a challenge for researchers.

For years, archeologists debated the location of the legendary "Vinland" visited by Erikson. Historical records, including a narrative written by German chronicler Adam of Bremen between 1073 and 1076, tell of "islands" discovered by the Norse, which early cartographers believed could be anywhere from St. Lawrence Bay to Cape Cod Bay to Chesapeake Bay. Others placed Vinland much closer to Europe, assuming it was perhaps simply a previously unknown part of Iceland.

But in 1960, a husband-and-wife team, Norwegian explorer Helge Ingstad and archeologist Anne Stine Ingstad, discovered the remains of Norse buildings at L'Anse aux Meadows in the Canadian province of Newfoundland. Between 1960 and 1968, the Ingstads uncovered the ruins of eight wood-framed buildings covered in sod and more than 800 Norse artifacts. Each building consists of a large hall alongside multiple rooms, with fireplaces, storage spaces, and workshops, and the entire settlement is believed to have housed up to 90 people. Carbon dating concludes that the site is approximately 1,000 years old, aligning with the time period that Erikson and his crew would have explored Vinland.

ABANDONED BUT NOT FORGOTTEN

Researchers speculate that L'Anse aux Meadows may be the site where Erikson's group established their base camp—the Leifsbúðir of the Saga of the Greenlanders and the Straumfjorðr of Erik the Red's Saga—and from there, they explored other areas near the Canadian coast. Since L'Anse aux Meadows is not known for its grapes or timber, the Vikings probably traveled south to eastern New Brunswick, a region with both grapes and impressive hardwood forests.

But is New Brunswick the famed "Vinland" the Vikings spoke of? So far, L'Anse aux Meadows is the only known Norse settlement in North America, although possible sites have been identified in Baffin Island, Labrador, and Prince Edward Island. New Brunswick, Nova Scotia, and Maine have been most often suggested as the "land of wine," but some researchers believe the "grapes" Erikson and his crew mentioned may have instead been wild berries, which could have been found in abundance at L'Anse aux Meadows.

The Norse settlement was only occupied for between 10 and 20 years. Many have wondered why the Vikings simply abandoned L'Anse aux Meadows and never returned to establish another colony, and the answer is probably a simple matter of numbers. The Norse population in Greenland was only around 400 to 500 at the time of Erikson's travels, and, considering the resources and risk required to journey to North America, it wasn't feasible or practical for the Vikings to attempt settling down in a new location. It made much more sense to merely continue exploring and settling in Europe, where resources were plentiful and political connections could be made.

Today, most archeologists use "Vinland" to refer to any area the Vikings visited in North America. Regardless of whether it was a specific location or not, Leif Erikson's discovery of the "land of wine" nearly 500 years before Christopher Columbus reached the Americas was an impressive accomplishment that reflected the curious nature of so many explorers who would follow his footsteps.

THE MOUND BUILDERS: MYTHMAKING IN EARLY AMERICA

In the early 1840s, the fledgling United States was gripped by a controversy that spilled from the parlors of the educated men in Boston and Philadelphia—the core of the nation's intellectual elite—onto the pages of the newspapers printed for mass edification. In the tiny farming village of Grave Creek, Virginia (now West Virginia), on the banks of the Ohio River stood one of the largest earthen mounds discovered during American expansion westward. The existence of these mounds, spread liberally throughout the Mississippi Valley, Ohio River Valley, and much of the southeast, was commonly known and had caused a great deal of speculative excitement since Europeans had first arrived on the continent. Hernando de Soto, for one, had mentioned the mounds of the Southeast during his wandering in that region.

MONEY WELL SPENT

The colonists who settled the East Coast noticed that the mounds, which came in a variety of sizes and shapes, were typically placed near excellent sites for villages and farms. The Grave Creek mound was among the first of the major earthworks discovered by Americans in their westward expansion. By 1838, the property was owned and farmed by the Tomlinson family. Abelard B. Tomlinson took an interest in the mound on his family's land and decided to open a vertical shaft from its summit, 70 feet high, to the center. He discovered skeletal remains at various levels and a timbered vault at the base containing the remains of two individuals. More importantly, he discovered a sandstone tablet inscribed with three lines of characters of unknown origin.

WHO WERE THE MOUND BUILDERS?

Owing to the general racist belief that the indigenous people were lazy and incapable of such large, earth-moving operations and the fact that none of the tribes who dwelt near the mounds claimed any knowledge of who had built them, many

19th-century Americans believed that the mound builders could not have been the ancestors of the Native American tribes they encountered. Wild and fantastic stories arose, and by the early 19th century, the average American assumed that the mound builders had been a pre-Columbian expedition from the Old World—Vikings, Israelites, refugees from Atlantis—all these and more had their champions.

Most agreed, however, that the New World had once hosted and given rise to a civilization as advanced as that of the Aztecs and Incas who had then fallen into disarray or been conquered by the tribes that now inhabited the land. Speculation on the history of the mound builders led many, including Thomas Jefferson, to visit mounds and conduct their own studies.

MORMONS AND THE MOUNDS

Meanwhile, the Grave Creek tablet fanned the flames of a controversy that was roaring over the newly established and widely despised Church of Jesus Christ of Latter Day Saints, founded by Joseph Smith. The Mormon religion is based upon the belief that the American continent was once inhabited by lost tribes of Israel who divided into warring factions and fought each other to near extinction. The last surviving prophet of these people, Mormon, inscribed his people's history upon gold tablets, which were interred in a mound near present-day Palmyra, New York, until they were revealed to fifteen-year-old Joseph Smith in 1823. Though many Americans were ready to believe that the mounds represented the remains of a non-indigenous culture, they were less ready to believe in Smith's new religion.

Smith and his adherents were persecuted horribly, and Smith was killed by an angry mob while leading his followers west. Critics of the Saints (as the Mormons prefer to be called) point to the early 19th-century publication of several popular books purporting that the earthen mounds of North America were the remains of lost tribes of Israel. These texts claimed that evidence would eventually be discovered to support their author's assertions. That the young Smith should have his revelation so soon after these fanciful studies were published struck many observers as entirely too coincidental. Thus, Abelard Tomlinson's excavation of the sandstone tablet with its strange figures ignited the passions of both Smith's followers and his detractors.

ENTER THE SCHOLAR

Into this theological, and ultimately anthropological, maelstrom strode Henry Rowe Schoolcraft, a mineralogist whose keen interest in Native American history had led to his appointment as head of Indian affairs. While working in Sault Ste. Marie, Schoolcraft married a native woman and mastered the Ojibwa language. Schoolcraft traveled to Grave Creek to examine Tomlinson's tablet and concluded that the figures were indeed a language but deferred to more learned scholars to determine just which language they represented. The opinions were many and varied—from Celtic runes to early Greek; experts the world over weighed in with their opinions. Nevertheless, Schoolcraft was more concerned with physical evidence and close study of the mounds themselves, and he remained convinced that the mounds and the artifacts they carried were the products of ancestors of the Native Americans. Schoolcraft's theory flew in the face of both those who sought to defend and those who sought to debunk the Mormon belief, and it would be more than three decades until serious scholarship and the emergence of true archeological techniques began to shift opinion on the subject.

ANSWERS PROPOSED, BUT QUESTIONS STILL ABOUND

History has vindicated Schoolcraft's careful and thoughtful study of the mounds. Today, we know that the mound builders were not descendants of Israel, nor were they the offspring of Vikings. They were simply the ancient predecessors of the Native Americans, who constructed the mounds for protection from floods and as burial sites, temples, and defense strongholds. As for the Grave Creek tablet: Scholars today generally agree that the figures are not a written language but simply a fanciful design whose meaning, if ever there was one, has been lost to the ages. Though the Smithsonian Institute has several etchings of the tablet in its collection, the whereabouts of the actual tablet have been lost to the ages.

THE IROQUOIS LEAGUE

Long before English settlers swarmed over the eastern coast of the "New World," Native Americans occupied the land around Lake Ontario now known as New York, as well as parts of New England, and parts of Canada. Sometime between the 14th and 16th centuries, the area became home to thousands of Indians in dozens of tribes.

THE HIGH FIVE

Five of these tribes experienced much intertribal fighting. According to legend, a wise sachem (chief) named Deganiwidah sought to make peace and foster goodwill among the nations through the efforts of another sachem named Hiawatha (no, not that Hiawatha). These five tribes—Seneca, Cayuga, Onondaga, Oneida, and Mohawk—sent 50 chiefs as a council and formed an alliance between 1500 and 1650 that came to be known as the "Five Nations of the Iroquois League." (A sixth nation, Tuscarora, joined in 1722.) Other names for this tribal organization were "the Woodland Democracy" and "the Iroquois Confederation."

Each tribe in the League had its own unique traits and qualities. The Seneca tribe—"People of the Great Hills"—was the largest, while the Cayuga, called "the Pipe People," was the smallest. The Onondaga were relatively peaceful and known as the "People of the Mountain." The Oneida—"People of the Standing Stone"—were pretty violent. The Mohawk, known as the "People of the Flint," were the fiercest of them all. Yet, the League had four moral principles to which they all agreed: a love of peace, respect for their laws, a sense of brotherhood, and a reverence for their ancestors.

A LONGHOUSE IS A HOME

Life in an Iroquois village was based on farming, even though the tribes did not have animals to help cultivate their fields. As such, many settlements were situated along rivers, where a spiral wooden fence surrounded the main buildings. These structures, known as "longhouses," could be anywhere from 30 to 350 feet long and were home for many, many families in individual living quarters under one roof (a somewhat primitive form of tenement housing). Several longhouses in an Iroquois village could house as few as 100 to as many as 3,000 people. A number of fires were kept burning in the middle of the longhouse, to provide heat in the winter months and allow cooking and baking year-round.

So strong was the concept of the longhouse in the Iroquois League, the tribes actually regarded their occupied land as one enormous longhouse. The Seneca considered themselves the "Keepers of the Western Door," and the Mohawk were the "Keepers of the Eastern Door" on the other end at the Atlantic Ocean. In between, the Onondaga were the "Keepers of the Fire," the Cayuga were the "Younger Brothers of Seneca," and the Oneida were the "Younger Brothers of Mohawk."

The social order of the League was matrilineal—women owned the longhouse, as well as garden plots and farming tools. They also set and maintained rules in the village and could appoint religious leaders. Women in the village were wholly responsible for daily life, as the men were seldom in camp. Their jobs—warfare, trading, trapping, and hunting— kept them away from the longhouse for months at a time.

MAKE WAR, NOT PEACE

Though the League claimed to have a "love of peace," they still engaged in many warlike activities. The Huron and

Algonquin tribes were natural enemies of the League, and tribal warfare was an important component of Iroquois society. The Mohawk were known for swift "hit-and-run" techniques of attack, wielding heavy tomahawk axes to kill their enemies and pillage their goods. But the League avoided large-scale war, remaining satisfied with small skirmishes of 20 to 30 warriors.

The League, as sophisticated as it may seem, lacked the social economics and organization to maintain standing armies and stage full-blown war with their enemies. Europeans joined the list of foes in the mid-1600s, as they landed in America and hunted beaver and other animals for pelts. As a result, the Iroquois were forced to move out into other territories for their prey, which increased their aggressive attacks.

Still, the Iroquois were masters of psychological warfare. They understood and exploited intimidation through kidnapping and torture, which instilled fear in others. Many captives were tortured, then assigned by the longhouse women as slaves to their families. Hideous instances of cannibalism were also common among the Iroquois. Jesuit priests like Jean de Brebeuf suffered such atrocities while attempting to minister their faith among the League nations.

The Iroquois League held many religious beliefs, including the power of medicine men. One group, known as the "False Face Society," donned fearsome carved wooden masks. They danced, shook turtle shells, and sprinkled ashes to bring about a cure for illness. A similar curing group, called the "Huskface Society," wore cornhusks as masks.

The League had much to offer in the way of operating a complex government body. The council of 50 sachems required that all decisions of the village had to be unanimous. If a sachem caused problems in the council, he was given three warnings. After that, he was ousted. Some historians believe that portions of the U.S. Constitution were based on the council of the Iroquois Confederacy. A curious visitor to many of the council meetings in the 1700s was a man named Benjamin Franklin. The Presidential Seal of America features an eagle holding 13 arrows—one for each original colony. Similarly, the Iroquois seal showed an eagle with five arrows in its talon—one for each nation. The Iroquois nations established peace and harmony with the United States, signing a treaty in 1794. Terms of the agreement endure to this day as, according to the 200-plus-year-old document, some nation members receive calico cloth as annual payment, while other tribes receive $1,800 a year.

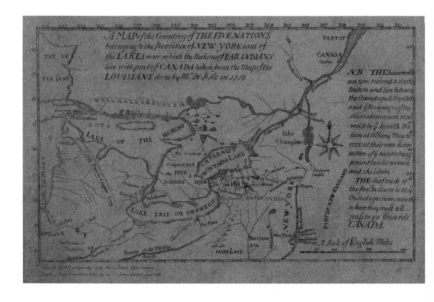

SOUTH AMERICA

CARAL-SUPE: THE FIRST AMERICAN CIVILIZATION?

The famous Pyramids of Giza are known not only as architectural wonders but as symbols of the ancient world. Their construction began around 2550 B.C., and the painstakingly assembled, precisely designed structures have astounded archeologists and tourists for centuries. The Egyptian pyramids, and the ancient peoples who built them, may be the first things that come to mind when we think of ancient civilization; but surprisingly, at the same time Egyptian kings were creating pyramids, another civilization was thriving on the other side of the world.

The Caral-Supe civilization, named after its location in the Caral region of Peru near the Supe River, was first discovered in 1905. But the site, believed to be relatively recent, drew little attention from researchers. Some scholars, however, including Peruvian anthropologist and archeologist Ruth Shady, weren't so sure that the site was as recent as many assumed. In 1996, Shady began excavations of the area, with the help of a couple dozen Peruvian soldiers.

AN EXCITING EXCAVATION

Working on a tight budget—sometimes even using her own money—Shady and her team of soldiers searched the ruins for the remains of pottery, which are often found at archeological sites. But strangely, there was none to be found. The absence of any pottery shards suggested an exciting possibility to Shady: these ruins, at first believed to be recent, were not just older than originally thought; they were also older than the creation of pot-firing technology in the area. If Shady's hunch was correct, it would mean that she was uncovering one of the oldest civilizations in the Americas.

It took several more years before Shady had the chance to prove her hypothesis. In 1999, she and her team uncovered a number of preserved bags woven from reeds while excavating a pyramid at the site known as Pirámide Mayor. Since the reeds were, at one time, living organisms, they were the perfect candidates for radiocarbon dating. Shady sent samples to be dated to researcher Jonathan Haas at the Field Museum in Chicago, and the results were exactly what she was hoping for: the reeds were 4,600 years old.

IMPRESSIVE ARCHITECTURE

Using other samples found in the region, Haas was able to definitively prove that the earliest city of the civilization, known as Huaricanga, dates back to 3500, B.C. But there is also limited evidence that humans may have been forming communities as early as 3700 B.C., and human activity in the area can be dated all the way back to 9210, B.C.

All of this evidence added up to an amazing understanding for archeologists: this pre-ceramic society, sometimes known as Norte Chico or simply Caral, was the oldest-known civilization in the Americas. At the same time the Egyptians were building their pyramids more than 7,000 miles away, the Caral-Supe peoples were creating their own immense architecture, including huge, terraced pyramids, sunken circular plazas with 30-foot-wide staircases, amphitheaters, atriums, and residential buildings.

FISH, COTTON, AND A TRADE AGREEMENT

In addition to the Supe River, the society relied on the Fortaleza and Pativilca rivers to provide irrigation in the arid climate. This access to water allowed the Caral-Supe peoples to grow a variety of edible plants like squash, beans, sweet potato, and guava. But researchers pondered these inland locations of the settlements, which were about 14 miles from the coast of Peru. Why did this civilization choose to live so far from the coastland, where oceanic sources of protein were abundant? Shady and her team excavated several items that provided clues, including pieces of achiote, a fruit found in the rain forest, and necklaces made from the seeds of the coca, a plant not found in the Caral region. Also discovered were remains of anchovies, sardines, and shellfish, which had to have come from the ocean miles away.

These items hinted that the Caral-Supe peoples enjoyed a thriving trade industry, one that allowed them to focus more on construction of their grand structures than on searching for food. Of course, this would mean that they must have possessed something of great worth with which to trade. More excavation at the site eventually uncovered the probable commodity: cotton. Shady discovered an abundance of cotton seeds and textiles in every area of the Caral-Supe site, leading the archeologist to conclude that the civilization must have traded cotton with other peoples in the region.

This would also serve to explain the presence of so many marine creatures at the site, even though it was so far inland. The Caral-Supe peoples probably traded their cotton to coastal fishermen, who needed the cotton to weave their fishing nets. In return, the fishermen provided Caral-Supe with plenty of seafood to supplement their mostly vegetarian diet, giving them vital access to protein. This relationship with the fishermen meant the Caral-Supe civilization was free to continue developing their infrastructure, without the need to be near the coast.

A MYSTERIOUS DECLINE

Over time, the Caral-Supe civilization would encompass a 35-square-mile area, including within its territory 17 different pyramid complexes. The largest of these, the Pirámide Mayor, measures 520 by 490 feet at the base, and rises 59 feet high. Aside from its impressive architecture, the civilization is notable not only for its lack of pottery of any kind, but also its lack of sculpture, carvings, paintings, or drawings. But while Caral-Supe may not have had any visual art, there is evidence that the peoples enjoyed musical arts. Many flutes made of pelican and condor bone have been uncovered at the site. At its height, the civilization is believed to have been home to more than 3,000 people, making Caral-Supe one of the most densely populated regions of the world at the time.

Sometime around 1800, B.C., the Caral-Supe civilization began to decline, for reasons that are unknown. Some of the structures appear to have been deliberately buried in an attempt to preserve them, suggesting the fall of the civilization didn't happen overnight. Researchers have noted that there is no evidence of warfare or violence in the location, so its disappearance is truly a mystery. But Caral-Supe's influence in the region is undeniable: the method of urban planning used by these ancient peoples was copied by other Andean civilizations for the next four thousand years. With ongoing research and excavation continuing at the site, the oldest civilization in the Americas may still one day provide us with answers to many questions.

CIUDAD PERDIDA: A CITY FOUND

The discovery of Ciudad Perdida is reminiscent of an adventure movie: In 1972, a group of treasure hunters stumbled upon a very old stone staircase hidden within the greenery of the Columbian jungle. When they climbed the stairs, they found themselves in an abandoned city, covered with vines and vegetation, which they called the "green hell." What they discovered was far from being a hell, however, as it became clear that their quest for treasure was successful. The site contained many gold figurines and valuable pottery, and the looters loaded up with goods to sell.

But when unusual gold and ceramic items began showing up on the black market, archeologists knew that something exciting had been found in the Columbian jungle. In 1976, researchers were finally able to find the elusive stone staircase in the jungle, and excavation of the abandoned city, now known as Ciudad Perdida, or "lost city," began.

NOT-SO-LOST CITY?

But "lost" may be a misnomer in the case of Ciudad Perdida. Local indigenous groups, including the Wiwa, Arhuaco, and Kogi tribes were all aware of the location of the city, and even visited it on occasion. But they preferred to keep it a secret, possibly hoping to prevent treasure hunters, such as the ones who eventually found it, from looting it.

The Kogi tribe helped researchers answer some of the questions posed by the existence of this city in the jungle. Built around A.D. 800, in the mountains of the Sierra Nevada de Santa Marta range, the city was one of many small villages inhabited by the Tairona people, who were the forebears of the Kogis. These villages were connected by stone pathways, not unlike the stone staircase that leads to the lost city. Within Ciudad Perdida, the largest of these villages, the Tairona people constructed more than 200 structures, including mountainside terraces, circular plazas, dwellings, storehouses, and ceremonial areas.

A LIFE UPENDED

For centuries, life on the mountain was simple and peaceful. Communities grew tomatoes, corn, avocado, pineapple, and guava, and, with a location close to the Caribbean Sea, were able to catch an abundance of seafood. The stone paths between villages allowed easy trade of food, textiles, pottery, and gold. Women and children wove fabric to create clothing and bags, and men were renowned as warriors and protectors.

But everything changed after the arrival of the Spanish conquistadors in the 1500s. Years of conflict and struggle followed, and although the Tairona men fought to resist the hostility of the Spaniards, they were not a naturally violent people. After even offers of gold failed to appease the conquistadors, the Tairona people were eventually forced to flee Ciudad Perdida, leaving it to be consumed by the jungle.

Today, tourists can visit this ancient city, which can still be described as "lost" for good reason: in order to reach it, visitors must trek for 27 miles through the jungle, crossing several rivers and enduring steep climbs. The journey takes at least two or three days, and a local guide must accompany all hikers for safety. While the hike requires payment of a fee, much of the money is used to preserve the site and protect it from overgrowth and looting, as well as ensures the indigenous peoples of the area have a say in how the site is run. For many visitors, the price is well worth it to have the chance to experience a bit of ancient history.

ANCIENT ARTISANS: MOCHE CULTURE

Spanning 250 miles of desert coastline in what is now Peru, the Moche civilization flourished between the first and eighth centuries, A.D. The culture is named after the Moche River valley, and the city of the same name is believed to have been the capital city of the peoples.

Until the 1980s, most of what archeologists knew about the Moche culture came from the city of Moche itself, located just south of Trujillo, the second-oldest Spanish city in Peru. Here, two large adobe structures have stood since around A.D. 450, known now as the *Huaca del Sol* and *Huaca de la Luna*—Temple of the Sun and Temple of the Moon. At one time, Huaca del Sol stood 164 feet high, with a base spanning 1115 feet by 524 feet. Researchers estimate that more than 130 million adobe bricks were used to construct the temple, which was the largest pre-Columbian adobe structure ever built in the Americas.

Sadly, almost two thirds of the original structure have been damaged or lost to erosion and looting. So, although Huaca de la Luna is the smaller of the two temples, it also has the good fortune of being better preserved, with faded murals that were once painted in bright colors still visible within the complex. Archeologists have also uncovered a large number of fine ceramic items, and they believe the two temples were once used for burials, as well as for administrative and religious purposes.

ELABORATE TOMBS, IMPRESSIVE POTTERY

While these two temples are impressive, archeological excavation beginning in the late 1980s gave researchers even more insight into the Moche culture. Dozens of platform pyramids were discovered, divided between two distinct regions known as Southern Moche and Northern Moche. The Southern region, which includes the Huaca del Sol and Huaca de la Luna, in believed to have been the center of Moche culture. The Northern region, centered around several valleys and rivers, was more independent and they probably had their own individual governments.

But the Southern and Northern Moche regions shared much of the same tradition and artwork, including an impressive variety of ceramics, textiles, and metalwork. The elites of society, such as royalty, warriors and priests, were buried in elaborate tombs covered in colorful artwork and filled with jewelry. These burial chambers were quite unique, as each was adjacent to a smaller compartment that offered a representation of the contents of the tomb, including a small copper figure to symbolize the deceased.

Moche artwork and pottery was some of the most sophisticated in the pre-Columbian era. The peoples used mold technology to create their wares, which included high-quality water jars and pots. These were painted, mostly with red and white colors, with scenes depicting people, animals, plants, or fantastical beings. Some of the scenes illustrated the more disturbing aspects of Moche life, including human sacrifice and the ritual consumption of blood. These practices were also evident at the temples, where numerous skeletons have been unearthed that show signs of violence and head trauma.

MASTERS OF METAL

The Moche are also renowned for their metalwork, which is considered some of the most impressive in the world. The civilization used highly advanced metalworking techniques, which have been difficult for even modern craftsmen to replicate. They invented or perfected many of the techniques themselves, using gold, silver, and copper to create sculptures, jewelry, headdresses, and metal plating for vases and pots. Archeological sites excavated in the late 1980s found a wealth of these metal objects in their original locations, leading researchers to conclude that the Moche metal artwork was often associated with the elite of society and the power they wielded.

But this power was finite, and for reasons unknown, the Moche civilization began to wane around A.D. 700. Scholars theorize that climate change may have played a role, with a period of intense rain and flooding followed by years of drought taking a toll on the society. Others believe earthquakes or encroaching sand dunes may have disrupted daily life, while some think social unrest and warring factions may have been the culprits. In all probability, a combination of these issues contributed to the downfall of the civilization. To this day, excavation continues and new discoveries await, ensuring the Moche will always hold an important place in the history of Peru and the ancient cultures of the world.

THE GOLDSMITHS: QUIMBAYA CULTURE

Located between what are now the cities of Cali and Medellin, Columbia, the valley of the Cauca River was home to the pre-Columbian Quimbaya civilization. Scholars estimate that the culture arose around the first century, A.D., and flourished between the years 300 and 600. Much is unknown about the Quimbaya peoples, and few direct descendants of the civilization remain. Even the Quimbaya language is considered extinct, adding to the mystery surrounding the culture's ancient existence.

With their tropical location, the Quimbaya peoples were able to grow a variety of food, such as corn, avocado, and guava. Archeologists have found evidence that they also hunted for food, and remains of animals like deer, rabbits, opossums, foxes, and others have been found. Funerals were important occasions to the Quimbaya, and they carefully constructed distinctive tombs for each person who was buried. Inside, the deceased was provided with food, weapons, personal items, and ceremonial objects, which were believed to be necessary for the next life.

TUMBAGA AND POPOROS

One of the civilization's main industries was the creation of textiles and cotton blankets. They also perfected a technique for extracting salt from the nearby river, and manufactured oil to be burned for lighting. Thanks to these resources, they enjoyed profitable trading relationships with neighboring regions.

But the Quimbaya's primary claim to fame has nothing to do with blankets, salt, or oil. Rather, it is their skill in metalwork, particularly gold, that has impressed scholars and art lovers worldwide. Gold was not terribly abundant in the Cauca River valley, so the Quimbaya developed a process to combine gold with copper into an alloy called *tumbaga*. Although the tumbaga was not pure gold, the alloy retained the brightness, beauty, and durability of the metal.

The most famous of the Quimbaya metal artifacts discovered by archeologists are called *poporos*. A poporo is a container with a long neck and a receptacle made to hold lime, which was made from powdered, roasted seashells. Indigenous cultures in Columbia, like the Quimbaya, used the lime during a sacred ritual called *mambeo*, in which coca leaves would be chewed along with the lime. To extract the lime from the container, a long metal pin was used. The poporos, and the mambeo ritual itself, were filled with symbolism and represented the idea of a dual god and the balance of opposites. The receptacle of the poporo symbolized femininity, while the long neck represented masculinity. The metallic pin joining with the lime was an illustration of the skies joining with the earth.

MUSEUM QUALITY

In addition to the poporos, Quimbaya artifacts include many
human figures made from both metal and clay ceramics. These
are often small figures, between 4 and 20 inches in height,
which were buried in tombs as companions for the deceased.
They also created an abundance of small animal and plant figures; necklaces, earrings, and other decorative ornaments; and
bowls, jars, and bottles. Some scholars believe that many of
the anthropomorphic and zoomorphic figures found are meant
to represent the gods worshiped by the Quimbaya, and the
bond they shared with nature.

While the Quimbaya civilization eventually faded away sometime after the tenth century, the plethora of artifacts they left
behind continues to mesmerize and educate history buffs.
The Metropolitan Museum of Art in New York contains many
Quimbaya items within its displays; but perhaps the most
impressive collection is located at the Museo del Oro, or the
Gold Museum, in Bogota, Columbia. Here, visitors can see the
famous Poporo Quimbaya, which was purchased from grave
robbers by the Banco de la Republica, the central bank of
Columbia, in the 1930s. In an effort to preserve this priceless
artifact and other pre-Columbian goldwork, the Gold Museum
was established in 1939, and now houses hundreds of Quimbaya artifacts as well as thousands of other pieces. The Poporo
Quimbaya has become a proud symbol of Colombia, and is a
testament to the intricate skill of the Quimbaya peoples.

THE KINGDOM OF QUITO

The Ecuadorian capital of Quito lies in a valley on the eastern slopes of Pichincha, an active volcano in the Andes Mountains. Sitting at an elevation of 9,350 feet, just under two miles above sea level, the city is the second-highest capital in the world, after La Paz, Bolivia. Officially, the city was established in 1534, which is the date Spanish conquistador Sebastián de Belalcázar founded it after defeating the Inca warrior Rumiñawi.

But Quito's history goes back much further than its official founding date. In fact, researchers have found evidence of human habitation in the region that dates back to 8000 B.C. American archeologist Robert E. Bell, while excavating a nearby extinct volcano in 1960, found tools made of obsidian glass left behind by hunter-gatherers. And in the Quito neighborhood of Cotocollao, researchers discovered the remains of a prehistoric village that once covered 64 acres. Burial sites, pottery, and stone figures were found near the ruins of ancient houses, which dated back to 1500 B.C.

THE CARA CULTURE

Sometime in the late 9th or early 10th century A.D., a civilization known as the Cara culture migrated from the coast of the Pacific Ocean up the Esmeraldas River to the area that is now Quito. After defeating the local Quitu tribe that inhabited the area, the Cara established a kingdom they called the Shyris, Scyris, or Caranqui civilization, but is now sometimes known as the Kingdom of Quito.

The kingdom was established in 980, and was ruled by a series of kings or tribal leaders, known as shyris, for almost 500 years. The Cara culture gradually spread into neighboring regions, building fortresses and leaving behind troops of fighters in each location. This was not without good cause: while the kingdom was the dominant culture in the region, it had not gained its place without making some enemies.

INCAN EMPIRE

In 1462, they were narrowly bested in a battle with an army led by Tupac Inca, the son of the emperor of the Incan Empire. Tupac Inca's son, Huayna Capac, built a capital city on what is today modern Quito, and the Cara culture, along with the Kingdom of Quito, was gradually absorbed into the Incan Empire.

When Sebastián de Belalcázar and the Spanish conquistadors arrived in 1534, the Incan general Rumiñawi decided he would rather see the city destroyed than fall into Spanish hands. He ordered the capital burned to the ground, destroying many artifacts of not only the Inca, but the Kingdom of Quito, as well. But recently, archeologists discovered 65-foot-deep Cara tombs found intact in the La Florida neighborhood of Quito. Efforts have been underway to preserve the artifacts found within and to learn more about the Cara culture. Perhaps one day we will have a much greater understanding of the civilization that once dominated Ecuador's mountainous capital city.

THE TIWANAKU OF BOLIVIA

Located near the Bolivian shore of Lake Titicaca, a freshwater lake in the Andes Mountains that straddles the border of Bolivia and Peru, the Tiwanaku archeological site was once the location of a culture that flourished more than a thousand years ago. For decades, scientists have debated the age of the site, with some believing it dates back to 1500 B.C. or even thousands of years earlier. But most researchers agree that the Tiwanaku culture first emerged sometime between 200 B.C. and A.D. 200.

Much of the confusion may stem from large amounts of looting and amateur excavations that occurred at the site starting shortly after the fall of Tiwanaku and continuing into the early 20th century. Some of the stones from the area were quarried for buildings and railroad projects, and structures were even used for target practice by the military. Needless to say, most of the buildings at Tiwanaku were destroyed by the time archeologists began studying and preserving the site. Luckily, the Bolivian government began restoring and protecting the area in the 1960s, and greater study of the site began in the late 1970s.

The archeological research at Tiwanaku has uncovered what was once an impressive civilization. The main structures at the site include the Akapana Pyramid, a rectangular enclosure known as the Kalasasaya, and a platform mound called the Pumapunku. These buildings, along with other reconstructed temples and courtyards, are open for public viewing.

PYRAMIDS, COURTYARDS, AND PLATFORMS

The Akapana is a platform mound or stepped pyramid, which is approximately 843 feet wide and 646 feet long, standing at about 54 feet tall. The mound was entirely manmade, consisting of large and small stone blocks mixed with dirt, which was excavated from the area. The pyramid was overlaid with a type of volcanic rock known as andesite, and stone blocks carved into puma and human heads were used to adorn the upper terrace. The largest of the andesite rocks is estimated to weigh more than 65 tons, suggesting the use of sophisticated construction practices.

The 300-foot-long Kalasasaya courtyard is notable for its monolithic "Gateway of the Sun," an arch which was discovered within the courtyard. The arch is carved with 48 squares, each representing what are thought to be angels or winged messengers. These messengers surround a central figure, a person holding staffs whose head is surrounded by rays, possibly representing the sun. Researchers theorize that the figure is meant to be either the god Viracocha, who was said to be the creator of the universe, sun, moon, and stars, or the god Thunupa, who was known as a "staff god" and controlled rain, lightning, and thunder.

The Pumapunku, similar to the Akapana, is a large manmade platform measuring approximately 549 feet long, 380 feet wide, and 16 feet tall. The structure is faced with megalithic blocks, and it also features a 22-foot-by-127-foot stone terrace that contains the largest stone block found within the Tiwanaku site, believed to weigh more than 144 tons.

SKILLED ARCHITECTS AND FARMERS

Many of the stones, carved figures, and other artifacts found at Tiwanaku were so intricately and precisely cut that some researchers have suggested that extraterrestrials may have had a hand in their creation! Of course, it is far more likely that the Tiwanaku themselves were very skilled architects. The stonework and arches found at the site seem to suggest that the civilization had a good grasp of descriptive geometry and may have been familiar with mathematical concepts like the Pythagorean Theorem.

For decades, researchers believed that Tiwanaku had been largely a ceremonial site. But archeological excavations in the late 20th century revealed a much different picture: that of a large and bustling metropolis that served as the capital city of a great civilization. The Tiwanaku civilization was especially knowledgeable about agriculture, which spurred a period of growth in the city between A.D. 300 and 700. They used a farming method known as the "raised-field system," consisting of raised planting areas separated by small irrigation canals. These canals helped to retain the heat of the sun even after it set, which was vital for keeping crops from freezing on cold nights. Farmers would also use the algae and plants that accumulated in the canals as fertilizer.

CONTINUED INFLUENCE

Tiwanaku grew to be very influential in the Andes, thanks in part to the civilization's agricultural economy. At its height, the city covered about one and a half square miles and had a population of between 10,000 and 20,000 people. Although the civilization disappeared around A.D. 1000, many believe that the Tiwanaku were the ancestors of the present-day Aymara indigenous peoples of the Andes and Altiplano regions of South America. The Tiwanaku also influenced many later cultures, including the Inca, and its impact was felt from what is now eastern and southern Bolivia to parts of Argentina, Chile, and Peru.

Today, researchers continue to make new discoveries in the area of Tiwanaku. Aerial photography, drones, and 3-D laser scanning have revealed more buildings that have yet to be excavated, including about a hundred circular and rectangular structures that are thought to be residential homes. Archeologists have even discovered artifacts and the ruins of a temple and part of a village submerged in Lake Titicaca, which were once a part of the city of Tiwanaku. And the civilization continues to contribute more to the contemporary world than just archeological finds: Farmers in Bolivia have recently started to use the Tiwanaku's raised-field system for their own crops, which has had a significant effect on increasing agricultural production. The Tiwanaku civilization is proof that even in modern times, we can continue to learn from our past.

THREADS OF AN ANCIENT CULTURE

When it comes to ancient artifacts, textiles are often a rare find. This is because the fragile organic materials used to create textiles like blankets and clothing have often been broken down over the centuries by temperature changes and weather conditions. By the time archeologists have discovered the remains of an ancient civilization, any textiles that once existed have been lost to the ravages of time.

But this is not true for the Wari civilization, which grew along the coast and in the highland areas of Peru between A.D. 600 and 1000. This culture is known particularly for its vibrant, intricate textiles, which were well-preserved thanks to their use in desert burials. The dry desert air helped to protect the numerous tapestries, hats, and tunics that have been discovered, which have given archeologists a glimpse into the artistic expression of this culture.

CAPITAL AND QUIPUS

But the Wari were far more than just prolific artists. Their civilization first began expanding from small villages in the Carahuarazo Valley of Peru and eventually established a capital at Huari, a city located 9,186 feet above sea level. Huari was spread out over almost six square miles, and at its height, had a population of about 70,000. The city was made up of densely packed rectangular buildings, usually two or three stories tall, which were divided into numerous rooms. Floors and walls were covered in plaster and painted white, and many buildings surrounded courtyards lined with stone benches. An underground network of conduits provided fresh water to the inhabitants of the city, which was said to be enclosed by stone and mortar walls up to 32 feet high and 13 feet thick.

Like many cultures before them, the Wari did not use any system of writing, so much of their social structure, political ideals, and other beliefs are unknown. However, the Wari did make use of *quipus*, which were recording devices made of knotted strings. The knots were used to represent numeric and other values, and were often used as calendars or to keep track of taxes, census data, or military information. While many other civilizations, including the Incan Empire, made use of quipus, many archeologists believe the Wari were the first to use the devices.

ARCHEOLOGICAL FINDS

While there may be a lack of written records, the Wari left behind quite a lot in the archeological record. Many structures have been identified at Huari, including a royal palace, a temple, and numerous residential buildings. Most are made of stone and mudbrick, and were once painted either white or red. More Wari ruins lie approximately 380 miles to the southeast, in Pikillaqta, which is believed to have been an administrative and military center. Access was limited to a single, winding pathway, and the city was laid out in a geometric pattern of squares. Dozens of artifacts have been uncovered at Pikillaqta, including small figurines made of stone, copper, gold, and semi-precious stones. These tiny figures, which are no more than two inches high, depict elite members of society such as shamans and warriors.

The figures found at Pikillaqta are just a small sample of Wari art that has been discovered. Archeologists have also found pottery and ceramics such as bowls, vases, and urns, and sophisticated metalwork items made of copper, silver, and gold. These include a silver face mask, breastplate, gold bracelets, and jewelry found in a royal tomb.

ABSTRACT ART

It is the tombs which have provided the greatest examples of Wari art, preserved in their textiles. Vibrant threads of red, yellow, orange, green, indigo, and blue were woven together to create stylized and often abstract depictions of plants, flowers, pumas, condors, and llamas. Staff god iconography is also often featured in these textiles. As their civilization progressed, the Wari's artistic expression became even more abstract, until it was often difficult to know what they were attempting to represent within the fabric. Researchers theorize this may have been a purposeful act by the elite, who wanted to control the interpretation of the symbols on each piece. Or it may have been a representation of the drug-induced visions the Wari sought during religious ceremonies.

Up to nine miles of wool and cotton thread was used for a single tunic, resulting in what can only be called wearable artwork. The abstract designs, which many art historians have likened to cubism and abstract expressionism, would have come alive as the wearer moved, walked, or ran, giving each textile a life of its own.

MODERN INSPIRATION

While the Wari's skill with irrigation had allowed them to withstand a drought in the 6th century that brought an end to the nearby Nazca and Moche civilizations, they were not so fortunate when drought returned in the 9th century. This time, the dry conditions lasted for centuries, and archeologists theorize that this is the probable cause of the Wari's decline. Many of their buildings were purposely destroyed and ritually buried, while others were kept intact but had deliberately blocked doorways. It may have been their intention to one day return, but the long-lasting drought offered inhospitable conditions for far too long. By A.D. 1000, the Wari had faded into obscurity.

But thanks to their vibrant, creative artwork, the Wari have not been forgotten. Many of their textiles and other artifacts are on display in museums around the world. Some researchers even believe that artists such as Georges Braque and Pablo Picasso were influenced and inspired by the artistry of Wari textiles. Without the artwork of this ancient civilization, it is possible that our own modern art would be lacking. After all, we never know how our actions, inventions, and creations will one day affect societies that do not yet exist.

LOST OR MYTHICAL?

THE PHILOSOPHER'S FABLE

The famous philosopher Plato is well-known for his "dialogues," literary prose in which two or more individuals discuss
moral and philosophical issues, often applying the Socratic
method. In two of these dialogues, *Timaeus* and *Critias*, composed around 360 B.C., the philosopher wrote of a land called
Atlantis, which he described as a huge island, "larger than Libya and Asia together," located somewhere beyond "the pillars
of Heracles." Atlantis, said to be a major naval power, attacked
Plato's concept of an ideal state, what he called "Ancient
Athens." But Athens successfully rebuked the Atlantean attack,
and the island fell out of favor with the gods. Eventually, the
entire civilization was destroyed by an earthquake, causing the
island to sink into the Atlantic Ocean.

Even though the tale of Atlantis has been told countless times
by numerous philosophers, writers, artists, and others, *Timaeus* and *Critias* are the only original sources of the story. Plato
himself claimed to have heard about the island from Solon, an
Athenian statesman and lawmaker, who visited Egypt sometime around 590 B.C. and heard about the history of Atlantis
from two priests in a temple at Sais. It would seem that the
Atlantis story is one of the earliest examples of "heard it from
a friend of a friend."

THE DEBATE BEGINS

But as unreliable as these sorts of stories may be, its origins did not stop Atlantis from immediately capturing the imaginations and igniting the curiosity of subsequent writers and thinkers. Some, like Plato's student Aristotle, believed the story to be nothing more than a fictional illustration of a philosophical idea. Others, like Crantor, a Greek philosopher who became a leader in Plato's Academy, were convinced that the existence of Atlantis was a historical fact. Some later historians and geographers, including Francis Bacon, Francisco Lopez de Gomara, and Alexander von Humboldt, believed that Plato was referring to the Americas when he described Atlantis. And the debate certainly didn't stop there. Today, the fact, or fiction, of Atlantis continues to be a topic of great interest and contention for everyone from historians and archeologists to avid readers and travel buffs.

But with no other records of Atlantis beyond Plato's fictional account, how did this mythical, ancient island become so well-known in our modern world? A 19th century Minnesota congressman named Ignatius Donnelly can take some of the credit. Donnelly was a bit of an amateur historian who dabbled in pseudoscience, and he had a theory about the achievements of the ancient world. He argued that knowledge of things like agriculture, language, and metallurgy must have originated with an earlier, but more evolved, society, since ancient civilizations were too primitive to have developed such skills on their own.

FLOODED OR FROZEN?

In 1882, Donnelly published a book called *Atlantis: The Antediluvian World*, in which he theorized that Atlantis may have been such an evolved society, and that all of civilization's advancements in knowledge and technology could be traced back to it. He suggested that the island, which he believed was once located in the Atlantic Ocean just outside the Strait of Gibraltar, was engulfed by shifting ocean waters during the Biblical Great Flood. In fact, *antediluvian* refers to the time period between the creation of the universe and the flood as described in the Book of Genesis. So, this "antediluvian" society, Donnelly argued, was the single origin of all great cultures in the world, where the Garden of Eden once flourished and humans rose from barbarism to civilized society.

While Donnelly's theory of Atlantis was eventually discredited by oceanographers, scientists, and even Charles Darwin, the book sold well and sparked renewed interest in the "lost" continent. Many believed that Donnelly's theory sounded plausible, especially since he placed Atlantis exactly where Plato said it should be: "The Pillars of Heracles" that Plato described are more commonly known as the Pillars of Hercules, the name given to the rock formations in Gibraltar and Morocco that mark the entrance to the Strait of Gibraltar.

Of course, with the advent of modern oceanography, scientists have been able to determine that there is no giant island beneath the waves of the Atlantic. But far from quelling interest in the story of Atlantis, its absence in the Atlantic only served to fuel more theories about the island. Some believe that Plato's story, while mostly fiction, may have been based on truth, and the real Atlantis is simply in another location. One theory, popularized by author Charles Hapgood in his 1958 book *Earth's Shifting Crust*, is that Antarctica was once Atlantis. Hapgood posited that the continent used to be located much further north than its present location, in a more temperate climate. But 12,000 years ago, the Earth's crust suddenly shifted, and Atlantis's civilized inhabitants faced extinction under Antarctica's layers of ice. In the 1970s, another author, Charles Berlitz, who wrote many books on paranormal phenomenon, suggested that Atlantis was, in fact, located in the Atlantic Ocean, but was a victim of the infamous Bermuda Triangle.

THE WRONG PILLARS?

More recently, some scholars have noted that before the 6th century B.C., the mountains on either side of the Laconian Gulf, in the southern Greek region of Peloponnese, were called the Pillars of Hercules. If Plato had been referring to these "pillars" in his writing, that would mean that Atlantis was more probably located in the Mediterranean Sea than in the Atlantic Ocean. Working off of this assumption, many researchers suggest that "Atlantis" may actually refer to the Minoan culture and the Thera eruption, which caused massive devastation to the civilization sometime between the 17th and 16th centuries B.C. Such a catastrophic disaster would have no doubt led to embellished stories about the society's downfall, which were passed down from generation to generation.

But most historians and archeologists believe that Plato's story was simply that: a story. Many even think that his claim to have heard the story from Solon in Egypt was part of his fabrication, since no evidence of the Atlantis story has been found in Egypt. But fabrication or not, the story of Atlantis has inspired countless works of literature, musical compositions, paintings, sculptures, and even comics. Perhaps this "lost" island is right where it should be: alive and well in the imaginations of dreamers everywhere.

THE ATLANTIS OF THE SANDS

In the Quran, a story is told about a tribe of people known as the Ad. The Adites built a powerful city filled with "lofty pillars," which rivaled any other city in Arabia. But the people turned their backs on Allah, living wicked lives and engaging in pursuits that displeased their God. A prophet named Hud was appointed by Allah to caution the Ad people to turn from their sinful ways, but they did not heed the warning. To punish the Adites, Allah sent a huge sandstorm that engulfed their city for seven nights and eight days. When it was over, the city, known as Iram of the Pillars, had vanished beneath the desert sands as if it had never existed.

Some people believe that the story of Iram is simply a parable, a morality tale that illustrates the dangers of living a selfish, arrogant life. But others are convinced that there is truth within the narrative, and the city of Iram may have once existed. For centuries, explorers, archeologists, and travelers have been fascinated by the possibility of a hidden city in the desert. Even famed army officer, diplomat, and archeologist T.E. Lawrence, known best by his nickname, Lawrence of

Arabia, was curious about Iram and its unknown location, dubbing it the "Atlantis of the Sands."

REIMAGINED EMBELLISHMENTS

While there are a few mentions of a place called Iram in some pre-Islamic poetry, the main source for the story of the city is the Quran. Over the centuries, the relatively simple tale in the religious text received embellishment in retellings. The "lofty pillars" of Iram were now covered in silver and gold, and encrusted with jewels, pearls, and saffron. What's more, the desert city was an oasis of flower gardens and trees, with abundant flowing rivers providing fresh water.

Perhaps the most detailed version of the story was found in *One Thousand and One Nights*, a collection of Middle Eastern folk tales that is also commonly known as *Arabian Nights*. Western audiences who were curious about the mystical, romantic land of Arabia were captivated by the stories when they were first translated into French in 1704, quickly followed by English, German, Italian, Russian, and other European languages. *One Thousand and One Nights* describes Iram as a city full of hundreds of splendid palaces, each one adorned with pillars, which took three hundred years to construct.

Some scholars argue that these elaborate, fanciful additions to the original story have prevented archeologists from taking the idea of a buried desert city more seriously. But others point out that the stories, especially the hugely popular *One Thousand and One Nights*, ignited an interest in explorers, travelers, writers, and researchers who otherwise would not have known about Iram. Whether it was jewel-encrusted or simply made of stone, many were determined to find this Atlantis of the Sands.

EVIDENCE IN THE DESERT?

In the 1970s, a discovery was made which helped to bolster the claim that Iram was at one time a real city. Italian archeologist Paolo Matthiae led an excavation of the ancient city of Ebla in northern Syria, where he and his team carefully uncovered houses, temples, walls, and gates that dated back to between 2500 and 2250 B.C. Also discovered were thousands of clay tablets and fragments of tablets containing Sumerian writing and cuneiform writing in a script now known as "Eblaite." And within these tablets, which seemed to describe nearby regions and cities that traded with Ebla, was the name Iram. Two decades later, in the 1990s, a team led by American filmmaker and amateur archeologist Nicholas Clapp excavated a location in Dhofar province of Oman. According to *The New York Times*, Clapp had made use of "ancient maps and sharp-eyed surveys from space" to uncover what he believed to be Ubar, another name for Iram of the Pillars. He discovered a large octagonal fort with tall towers, which had partially collapsed when it fell into a sinkhole.

STILL SEARCHING

While the site is located within the Rub' al Khali desert, also known as the "Empty Quarter," the area most often suggested as the location of Iram, the ruins of the fort are also believed to be on what used to be a trade route for frankincense. The site is located at Shisr, which was known for its large well, the only source of water within several days' journey, and, therefore, a logical choice to establish a town. Archeologists also believe that the city discovered by Clapp was not destroyed by a sandstorm, but rather by the sinkholes that once housed the area's well water. The Saudi Arabian press was also critical of the find, insisting that similar "lost" cities had been uncovered in the country's deserts and were better contenders for the title of Iram.

To date, no city has been discovered in the Arabian desert that truly fits the many descriptions of Iram of the Pillars, whether ordinary or fanciful. While many researchers believe that the city is entirely mythical, others are still convinced that the city of Iram and the Ad people who once occupied it were quite real. With around 250,000 square miles of desert to explore, it is possible that Iram of the Pillars is still out there, sleeping beneath the sands, waiting to be found.

OUT OF THE MIST

In 1674, a man named W. Hamilton from Derry in Northern Ireland wrote his cousin a letter in which he described an incredible tale. Hamilton wrote of a ship captain named John Nisbet who sailed from Ireland with a small crew of men to transport butter, tallow, and animal hides to France. After dropping off their cargo, they filled the ship with French wines and headed back to Ireland. But a couple days into their return journey, a thick fog enveloped the ship, making navigation difficult. When the fog lifted after a few hours, the sailors found themselves just offshore of an unknown island, with a strong wind pushing the ship perilously close to rocks. In order to get their bearings and avoid running aground, they decided to drop anchor until the wind died down.

Several sailors went ashore to explore the mysterious island, hoping to get an idea of where they were. Animals, including horses, cows, sheep, and rabbits, roamed the green hills, but not a single human, or even a house, was seen. But strangely, the group soon happened upon an old castle, which seemed to be the only structure on the island. The men knocked on the door of the castle incessantly, but no one answered and no sound came from within. Assuming the castle, and perhaps even the entire island, was abandoned, the men made their way back to the shore, describing to Captain Nisbet what they'd found. Since it would soon be dark, the company of sailors gathered wood and built a huge bonfire on the beach, where they sat warming themselves as night fell.

END OF AN EVIL CURSE

Suddenly, a terrifying sound erupted from the woods, seemingly emitted from somewhere near the old castle. The sailors immediately abandoned the fire and made their way back to the ship, where they hid in fear all night. When they ventured outside the next morning, they were startled to see a very old man leading a group of people toward the ship. When Captain Nisbet and his crew went ashore to greet them, the old man and his group began enthusiastically hugging the very confused sailors. The old man told them that his ancestors had lived on the island for centuries, ruling as princes. But an evil necromancer had imprisoned dozens of important citizens inside the castle, and hidden the island from the eyes of mortals, for a period of one hundred years.

When the one hundred years had passed, the island again became visible to human eyes, as Captain Nisbet and his crew had discovered. But the people in the castle were doomed to be imprisoned until fire had been kindled upon the island. When the sailors made their bonfire, the curse was finally lifted, and the horrible sound of the necromancer's departing evil washed over the island. The freed captives thanked the sailors profusely, offering them some of the gold and silver that were mined on the island. The island, the old man told Captain Nisbet, was known as O'Brazile, and it was not far from the sailors' home in Ireland.

AN UNAPPROACHABLE ISLAND

While Hamilton's story is quite fanciful—in fact, most historians agree is it a work of fiction created by Irish playwright Richard Head—it is not the only story of this mysterious vanishing island. Sometimes also known as *Breasal, Brazil, Brasil,* or most commonly *Hy-Brasil,* this island began appearing on maps in 1325, usually off the western coast of Ireland. Irish folklore claimed it was visible for only one day every seven years, otherwise it was perpetually shrouded in fog. But over the centuries, many sailors claimed to have seen the mysterious Hy-Brasil, some even claiming they were close enough to make out features of the island. One ship captain insisted he saw a harbor, but when he attempted to sail toward it, a mist rolled in and he was unable to reach the shore.

Despite these accounts, most historians agree that Hy-Brasil never actually existed. But that doesn't explain why so many centuries of maps featured the island. It was called *Insula de Brasil* on a chart created by Venetian cartographer Andrea Bianco in 1436. In 1562, Spanish cartographer Diego Gutierrez named it *Isola de Brazil*. French cartographer Guillaume de L'Isle named the island *Rocher de Brasil*, or Brasil Rock, on a map published in 1769. Hy-Brasil kept appearing on maps until 1872, when it was last depicted on a British admiralty chart.

GONE BUT NOT FORGOTTEN

Most scholars believe that the island was included on these maps simply due to hearsay. Rumors of Hy-Brasil's existence reached the ears of mapmakers, who included the mysterious island on their charts, even though there was no evidence that it was real. But not all cartographers believed the rumors: In 1753, British cartographer Thomas Jeffreys did include the island on a map, placed just southwest of Ireland. But he labeled the island the "Imaginary Island of O Brazil."

It's easy to assume that the appearance of "phantom islands" on maps is an issue from a bygone era. But a nonexistent island named Sandy Island, once said to be near the French territory of New Caledonia, was charted on maps from 1774 all the way up until 2012. In that year, an Australian marine research ship passed through the area and confirmed that the island did not exist, finally resulting in Sandy Island's removal from maps. While Hy-Brasil may have met the same fate, its exclusion from geographical charts has not quelled the interest in its legend. This mysterious island, shrouded in mist, will continue to be a fascinating part of Irish culture.

THE MAGICAL, MYSTICAL BUYAN

Russian folklore tells the tale of Koschei, a hero, or sometimes anti-hero, who cannot be killed. Often called "Koschei the Immortal" or "Koschei the Deathless," he hides his soul, or, as some tales call it, "death," within nested objects to keep himself safe. In one particular tale, Koschei's soul is tucked away in a needle, which is placed inside an egg, which is then hidden in a mystical oak tree. The location of the tree provides even more security, for it stands on the magical island of Buyan, which has the ability to appear and disappear with the movement of the oceanic tides.

Said to be the "Slavic Atlantis," Buyan was considered a sacred place to ancient Slavs, who believed the island to be the first land to appear from the primordial ocean. While some say it is located beneath the water, others believe it is merely invisible to mortal eyes. It is also thought to be the source of all weather, where Perun, the god of the sky, rain, thunder, and lightning, sends forth whatever conditions he deems fit for the season. In addition to Perun, the island is said to be home to two sun goddesses called Zoryas, who represent the morning star and the evening star, as well as three brothers: the eastern, northern, and western winds.

MAGICAL STONES, MYTHICAL CREATURES

The island of Buyan is also known for the *Alatyr,* a brilliant white stone carved with sacred letters, possessing magical properties. Sometimes called "father to all stones," "the stone

261

of all stones," or "the navel of the world," the Alatyr is said to mark the center of the universe, and anyone who finds it may be granted healing and happiness. But the stone is not left unattended: it is guarded by a wise serpent named Garafena, who is often called upon in incantations to protect against snake bites, and a bird called Gagana, who sports an iron beak and copper claws. Gagana is a mystical bird who can not only tell the future, but can also work miracles for those who ask.

Garagena and Gagana are not the only fantastical creatures on Buyan. The island is also home to the Indrik, a strange beast with the body of a bull, head of a horse, legs of a deer, and the single horn of a unicorn. Indrik is the caretaker for underground water sources, as well as the protector of other animals. As he moves around underground, he causes the earthquakes that occur on Earth.

And lurking somewhere in the darkness on Buyan is Koschei, who is usually portrayed as an old, hunched man, with long gray hair and a beard. But his appearance is deceiving, because while he seems weak, this nature spirit is quite powerful, ruling the darkness and controlling the souls of the dead. It is said that Koschei can fly through the air, borne by dark clouds, thunder, and lightning, and can shape-shift into the form of a whirlwind. In many folktales, Koschei has the ability to change his voice as well, using his charming talk to seduce the brides of his enemies. And while it may be difficult to kill this "immortal" and "deathless" spirit, it is not impossible. One need only find the large oak tree on Buyan island where Koschei has hidden his soul. Once Koschei's soul is possessed by another, the spirit begins to weaken, grows sick, and eventually loses all his magical power.

AN AIR OF TRUTH?

The stories of Buyan and its mystical, magical creatures seem to make it obvious that this island is nothing more than fiction. And yet, some historians believe that the island has roots in a real place. The German island of Rügen, located in the Baltic Sea, is most often suggested as the location of the mythical Buyan. This island, Germany's largest, was once the location of a West Slavic tribe called Runi. In the 7th century, the Runi built a prosperous civilization on Rügen, where they worshiped the god Svantevit, a war god, supreme deity, and father to other gods. But in the 12th century, the Danish took over the island, destroying the temples and worship sites of the Runi. Today, ruins of these pagan sites, as well as Runi residential buildings, are still found on the northern part of island, and many believe that the Runi culture was the inspiration for many of the stories about Buyan.

Whether the stories of Buyan were inspired by a real place or are simply figments of active imaginations, we may never know. But the enduring tales of Koschei, Garagena, Gagana, and the Alatyr stone have ensured that Buyan, wherever it is, will never be forgotten.

HOUSE OF THE ROUND TABLE

In the 12th century, British cleric Geoffrey of Monmouth helped to ignite interest in the famous King Arthur, mentioned in his book, *Historia regum Britanniae*, or *The History of the*

Kings of Britain. But while Geoffrey may have brought the valiant king to the world's attention, he never mentioned a detail that is now synonymous with King Arthur: the castled city of Camelot, where Arthur held court.

In fact, the first mention of Camelot didn't come from Great Britain at all, but rather France, in a late-12th century poem written by Chrétien de Troyes. In the poem, entitled *Lancelot, the Knight of the Cart*, the castle is merely mentioned in passing, giving no hint of the significance it would soon play in King Arthur's legend. Chrétien, like Geoffrey, placed King Arthur's main court in Caerleon in Wales, with many minor courts in various other cities and castles. But in the 13th century, French romances began embracing Camelot as King Arthur's seat of power. These literary texts, known as the Vulgate and Post-Vulgate cycles, were written by an unknown author or authors and are composed of thousands of pages of texts. The stories contain hundreds of characters from King Arthur lore, engaging in various exploits that are woven together throughout the manuscripts. One story calls Camelot, "the city most full of adventures," and talks of a land filled with magicians, dragons, giants, and knights.

THE KING AND HIS KNIGHTS

According to a Vulgate story, Camelot was founded by Joseph of Arimathea, who was also said to have founded the Glastonbury Abbey, believed by some to be the final resting place of King Arthur. Joseph established the Church of St. Stephen the Martyr in the middle of the city, which would be Camelot's largest church. While the city was small, at times requiring visitors to shelter in tents and pavilions in the nearby forests and meadows, it still had plenty of space for knightly tournaments, which were a regular occurrence. It was also well fortified, surviving several wars against the Saxons.

In the 5th or 6th centuries, King Arthur held court in a castle in Camelot, which was said to be located near a body of water. The castle had a hall for feasts, many bedrooms, and a main courtyard, but the most famous feature of the castle was the Round Table. The table was said to have been a wedding gift from King Leodagan of Carmelide, the father of Guinevere, King Arthur's wife. The table was so massive that 150 knights, who were entrusted with protecting the peace of Camelot, could fit around it. These included such familiar names as Lancelot, Galahad, Percival, and Gawain, among dozens of others. The Round Table, having no corners and therefore no head, was a symbol of the equal status of all participants in King Arthur's court.

By the end of the Vulgate stories, nearly every knight of the Round Table, despite their strength and bravery, was dead, as was King Arthur. While Camelot survived for a short time, eventually it was attacked by King Mark of Cornwall, who was once defeated in battle by Arthur and his knights. The people of Camelot, lost without their valiant protectors, were quickly defeated, and King Mark destroyed not only the city, but also the Round Table.

To the 13th-century readers of the Vulgate stories, it would have been evident that Camelot, if such a place had been real, no longer existed. But over the centuries, the legend of Camelot has been retold many times, with both King Arthur's story and the stories of his grand city reimagined and reinterpreted. Some even believe that Camelot was a real place, and perhaps King Arthur was a real person.

EXCAVATIONS AND EVIDENCE

Several places have been suggested as possible locations of what was once Camelot. One of the most popular candidates is Cadbury Castle, an Iron Age hillfort in Somerset County, England, which was proposed by poet and antiquary John Leland in 1542. Leland was convinced that King Arthur was a historical figure and not a fictional character, and his theory that Camelot was once located at Cadbury Castle prompted archeological digs in the area in the 20th century. Excavations revealed evidence of human occupation of the area from the 4th millennium B.C. until the 6th century A.D., and ruins of a large building, possibly a great hall, were found. Cadbury Castle is also located not far from Glastonbury Tor, which some believe is where King Arthur is entombed.

Another Camelot contender is Tintagel Castle, a historic site perched on the cliffs of Cornwall. According to Geoffrey of Monmouth, King Arthur was born in this location. In the 1980s, slate tablets with Latin inscriptions were discovered at Tintagel which mentioned "a descendant of Coll," which some researchers believe refers to King Coel, said to be one of Arthur's ancestors. Excavations at the site have uncovered pottery dating back to the 5th and 6th centuries, lending more credence to the site's possible history as Camelot; however, the castle ruins that now stand at the site date back only to the 1100s.

Many other locations have been associated with King Arthur and have been posited as potential Camelot sites, but most scholars agree that the accounts of the city and its king are entirely fictional. But that hasn't stopped the theories and speculation from persisting into modern times. Camelot has inspired poems, songs, movies, television shows, a famous Broadway musical, and was even used to describe the presidency of John F. Kennedy. Kennedy was said to have been particularly fond of a line in the finale of the musical: *Don't let it be forgot/ That once there was a spot/ For one brief, shining moment/ That was known as Camelot.* Whether it was real or imagined, the memory of this legendary city, the knights who protected it, and its famous king will not soon be forgotten.

Evidence or not, the idea of Glastonbury Tor as Avalon persists today. Tourists from all over the world visit the site and the purported resting place of King Arthur. But perhaps Avalon was never meant to represent a physical location. Some believe that stories of Avalon are meant to mirror stories of an afterlife, or a portal to another realm, where magic and otherworldly beings reside. Brave King Arthur and magical Avalon may not be a part of this world at all, but rather a part of a world yet unknown and unseen.

KINGDOM BENEATH THE SEA

Standing at Land's End, near the town of Penzance in Cornwall, England, one might assume that the rocky cliff is, indeed, the end of the world. Sitting at the westernmost point on mainland England, the granite promontory is popular with tourists seeking the calm sounds of ocean waves as well as rock climbers looking for an adrenaline rush. But according to Arthurian legend and the tragic story of *Tristan and Iseult*, Land's End wasn't an end at all. Rather, it marked the beginning of a stretch of land known as the kingdom of Lyonesse.

According to legend, Lyonesse spanned the area between Cornwall and the Isles of Scilly 30 miles away in the Celtic Sea, and was the home to Tristan, one of the Knights of the Round Table. Tristan's father, Meliodas, was the king of Lyonesse, and his son was next in line for the throne. When the king died, Tristan was at his uncle's court in Cornwall, which turned out to be fortuitous; because on the night of November 11 in either the year 1089 or 1099, the kingdom of Lyonesse sank beneath the sea, never to be seen again.

A GIANT WAVE AND A SOLE SURVIVOR

But before its catastrophic destruction, Lyonesse was said to be home to a race of strong, hardy people who worked the fields and low-lying plains of fertile soil in the kingdom. They were particularly fond of churches, and built 140 in total, including a grand cathedral that sat on what is now the Seven Stones reef located halfway between Cornwall and the Isles of Scilly.

But despite their apparent devotion to religion, Celtic lore tells of a grave crime or transgression committed by the people of Lyonesse that resulted in a swift and terrible punishment from God. In the dead of night, a ferocious storm rolled in, pummeling the kingdom with winds and rain. But the final blow was dealt by a massive tsunami wave, which engulfed Lyonesse and wiped it off the Earth.

The stories of Lyonesse never mention what terrible crime was committed by the people of the kingdom, but many liken the legend to the Biblical story of Sodom and Gomorrah. According to that story, Lot and his two daughters survived the destruction sent by God. And according to the story of Lyonesse, a single man, usually called Trevelyan, survived the wave that destroyed the city.

The man had been out hunting and fallen asleep under a tree, only to be awoken by the sounds of the gigantic wave crashing into the kingdom. He jumped onto his white horse and galloped for higher ground. The horse ran so quickly that it lost a shoe, and the pair barely made it to what is now Land's End.

Today, several families in Cornwall claim to be descendants of Trevelyan and use family crests featuring either horseshoes or a white horse. But beyond the stories that have been passed down from previous generations, there is no evidence to suggest Lyonesse ever existed. Still, locals insist that on days when the sea is calm, the sound of church bells can be heard off the coast of Land's End, ringing from their resting place beneath the sea.

THE AMAZONS

They were the epitome of girl power—fierce mounted warriors who often emasculated the best male fighters from other societies. They were the Amazons—man-eaters of the ancient world. The ancient Greeks were enthralled by them. Greek writers, like today's gossip columnists, relished lurid tales of love affairs between Amazon queens and their Greek boy toys. Others wrote of epic battles between Amazon warriors and the greatest heroes of Greek mythology. Given their prominent place in Greek lore, the story of the Amazons has generally been considered the stuff of legend. But recent archeological finds suggest that a race of these warrior über-women may have existed.

THE AMAZONS ACCORDING TO THE GREEKS

History's first mention of the Amazons is found in Homer's *Iliad*. Homer told of a group of women he called *Antianeira* ("those who fight like men"), who fought on the side of Troy against the Greeks. They were led by Penthesilea, who fought Achilles and was slain by him. According to some accounts, Achilles fell in love with her immediately afterward. Achilles was highly skilled in the art of warfare, but it seems he was sorely lacking in the intricacies of courtship. From then on, the Amazons became linked with the Greeks. Their very name is believed to derive from the Greek *a-mazos*, meaning "without a breast." This referred to the Amazon practice of removing the right breast of their girls so that they would be unencumbered in the use of the bow and spear. This may have made Greek, Roman, and European artists a bit squeamish because their depictions of Amazons showed them with two breasts, though the right breast was often covered or hidden.

According to Greek mythology, the Amazons were the offspring of Ares, god of war. Though the Amazons may have had Greek roots, they didn't want anything to do with them. The Amazons established their realm in a land called Pontus in modern-day northeastern Turkey. The Greeks paint a picture of the Amazons as a female-dominated society that banned men from living among them. In an odd dichotomy between chastity and promiscuity, sexual encounters with men were taboo except for once a year when the Amazons would choose partners from the neighboring Gargareans for the purpose of procreation. Female babies were kept; males were killed or sent back with their fathers. Females were raised to do everything a man could do.

SOAP OPERA ENCOUNTERS WITH GREEK HEROES

The Greeks and Amazons interacted in a love-hate relationship resembling something from a soap opera. Hercules, as one of his labors, had to obtain the girdle of Amazon queen Hippolyte. He was accompanied in his task by Theseus, who stole Hippolyte's sister Antiope. This led to warfare between the Greeks and Amazons as well as several trysts between members of the two societies. One account has Theseus and Antiope falling in love, with her dying by his side during a battle against the Amazons. Another account has Theseus and Hippolyte becoming lovers. Stories of Hercules have him alternately wooing and warring with various Amazonian women.

Jason and the Argonauts met the Amazons on the island of Lemnos. Completely unaware of the true nature of the island's inhabitants, Jason queried the Amazons as to the whereabouts of their men. They told him their men were all killed in an earlier invasion. What the Argonauts didn't realize was that the Amazons themselves were the killers. The Amazons, anticipating another opportunity for manslaughter, invited the Argonauts to stay and become their husbands. But Jason and the boys, perhaps intimidated by the appearance of the Amazons in full battle dress, hightailed it off the island.

MORE THAN MYTH?

Herodotus perhaps provides the best connection of the Greeks to what may be the true race of Amazons. Writing in the 5th century B.C., Herodotus chronicles a group of warrior women who were defeated in battle by the Greeks. They were put on a prison ship, where they happily went about killing the Greek crew. Hellcats on land but hopeless on water, the women drifted to the north shores of the Black Sea to the land of the Scythians, a nomadic people of Iranian descent. Here, says Herodotus, they intermarried with the Scythians on the condition that they be allowed to keep their traditional warrior customs. They added a heartwarming social tenet that no woman could wed until she had killed a man in battle. Together, they migrated northeast across the Russian steppes, eventually evolving into the Sarmatian culture, which featured a prominent role for women hunting and fighting by the sides of their husbands.

Though the Amazons are mostly perceived as myth, recent archeological discoveries lend credence to Herodotus's account and help elevate the Amazons from the pages of Greek legend to historical fact. Excavations of Sarmatian burial grounds found the majority of those interred there were heavily armed women, all of whom got the very best spots in the site.